Bon Appetit!

ZOV

RECIPES AND MEMORIES FROM THE HEART
by Zov Karamardian

TEXT COPYRIGHT © 2005 BY ZOV KARAMARDIAN

PHOTOGRAPHS COPYRIGHT © 2005 BY PORNCHAI MITTONGTARE
FOOD STYLING BY BASIL FRIEDMAN
PROP STYLING BY MAGGIE WARD
BOOK DESIGN BY TOM TOR

LIBRARY OF CONGRESS CATALOGING-IN-PUBLICATION DATA AVAILABLE

ISBN 0-9759558-0-2
10 9 8 7 6 5 4 3 2 1

FIRST EDITION

ZOV'S PUBLISHING, LLC
17440 E 17TH ST. TUSTIN, CA 92780 U.S.A
PHONE: 1-800-980-ZOVS (9687)
WWW.ZOVS.COM
WIMMER COOKBOOKS

I dedicate this book with love to my mother, my husband Gary, my son Armen, and my daughter Taleene. Without their patience, encouragement, and love, this book would not have been possible. I'd also like to dedicate my first cookbook to the memory of Julia Child, a dear friend and mentor whom I miss terribly.

CONTENTS

FOREWORD BY DEAN KOONTZ

The joy of food. This is one of the greatest gifts of civilization and a free society: We enjoy sufficient prosperity and have enough leisure time to elevate cooking into *culinary art*. Some of us have so little kitchen knowledge that making toast is a challenge, but we watch the Food Network and wish we could be wizards with a whisk. Others are so talented that they are amateur chefs only because no one pays them for their fine cooking. Zov Karamardian has long been an inspiration to serious foodies, both to those who work wonders in their home kitchens and to those of us who wish we had the knowledge, tools, and talent to do more than boil water.

Publishers Weekly, the trade magazine of the publishing industry, once asked me to name and describe my three favorite restaurants in Orange County. My selections were to be recommended in an article aimed at 25,000 book-industry people attending a convention here. I began by speaking effusively of Zov's Bistro, especially noting that in years of steady patronage and perhaps (at that time) a thousand dinners, I had *never* been served anything less than a splendid meal. As I made this statement to the reporter, I realized how astonishing it was for any restaurant both to serve food of exceptionally high quality and to do so with such unfailing consistency. By now, we have eaten at Zov's on perhaps two thousand occasions, and I *still* have had no reason for complaint.

I admire Zov Karamardian as a person and as a chef, but also as a businesswoman. The unique concept of her restaurant, the diligence with which that concept is fulfilled and constantly refreshed, the exceptional service, the relaxed yet sophisticated ambiance, the genuine friendliness of the staff—each of these achievements results not solely from Zov's passion for the culinary arts but also from her sound business sense and her talent for management, two qualities that one does not always associate with people who are also highly creative.

When I've had a productive day writing or have received good news from my agent and publisher, dinner becomes a quiet celebration. When the writing doesn't go well or the news is bad, the atmosphere of Zov's restaurant and the food she serves remind me that joy is to be found everywhere in life, even on lousy days, and dinner once more becomes a celebration not of the day just passed but of the one ahead.

Now Zov has written this volume to make it possible for us to experience her acclaimed cuisine at home. She has developed recipes with her signature richness and complexity of flavor that can be undestood and successfully followed by both those of you who are gifted home cooks but also by those--like me—who are culinarily challenged. This is a book rich not only with a love of food but with a love of life, family, and tradition. Between these covers is the essence of civilization and a guide to the civilized life.

ACKNOWLEDGEMENTS

I am blessed and fortunate to be able to work each day with my family. My husband Gary, my son Armen, my daughter Taleene, and my amazing mother Araxi give me their undying love and support as well as their talents; their contribution to the success of Zov's Bistro. Having them with me in the restaurant makes me realize the value of having a vision and pursuing it with passion, generosity, and love.

This book could not have been completed without the continued support of so many talented and loving friends, colleagues, and family members.

Special thanks to my writing coach, Paige Davis, who taught me to find my voice and motivated me to see myself as a writer. Without you, this book would never have been possible.

I would also especially like to thank Frank Groff, my publicist, for supporting my dream of Zov's Cook Book and believing in my ability to create the dream.

My deep appreciation goes to my photographer, Pornchai Mittongtare, for his artistic vision and his direction, assembling a dedicated team for this project. Pornchai is one of the very best food photographers in the industry, not only because he has an amazing eye, but also because he visually captures the most tantalizing essence of every dish. A big thank you to David Kiang, Pornchai's assistant.

Sincere thanks to Tom Tor, for his wonderful sense of humor and excellent direction of his design team. Thanks to all of them for their creative talent, vision, and cutting-edge design.

To Basil Friedman and his assistant, Marcella Capasso, who "styled" the food with mouth-watering effect. To Maggie Ward, our prop stylist who made sure each dish looked better than the one before. Ultimately to Rochelle Palermo-Torres, for testing and editing each recipe and then lending her invaluable advice to insure that each recipe was perfect. Rochelle you are the best! Last but not least, a big thank you to Kathryn Bold, for being part of the copy editing team of my book.

A special thanks to the team at Melissa's Produce for finding the freshest fruits and vegetables -- even if that means searching the four corners of the earth. (When we needed pomegranates, Melissa's found the only two cases available in the United States.)

Finally, I must thank one of the world's finest pastry chefs, Michelle Bracken, whose talent and skill are unrivaled. A special thanks to my very talented head cook Elias Estrada, who works harder than anyone I know. Many thanks to my management team and the entire staff at Zov's Bistro —you are all amazing! Thank you so much.

INTRODUCTION

Great cooking stems from experimenting with readily available fresh foods, herbs, and spices—the kind of ingredients you can find in your local supermarket. It's all about convenience and innovation. That's the philosophy of my book "Zov!"

Many recipes in this cookbook reflect dishes I learned from my mother, grandmother, and innumerable generous people I've met during my world travels. They contain the seeds of my Armenian heritage, yet they're influenced by many` cultures and styles. The recipes fuse traditional techniques and flavors with modern trends in cooking to yield unique and delicious dishes.

In 1959, I began to appreciate the difference that cooking with good, fresh ingredients can make. On the first day I arrived in America from the Middle East, my father's cousins took me to a supermarket in New York City. I had never seen a supermarket before. In the Middle East, everything was sold in the souks— bustling, open-air marketplaces that never seemed to close. The merchants there displayed bins of beautiful fruits and vegetables—apples, lemons, pears, berries, pomegranates, apricots, all ripe and full—but they wouldn't let us touch them. After we would place our order, someone would emerge from the back of the stalls with our bags of fruit, but they weren't the lush items displayed in the bins. Instead of beautiful apples, they'd give us inferior ones!

In the American supermarket, I actually got to touch the finest fruits and vegetables. I could explore the textures and shapes of such unimaginable foods as pineapples. I got to lift a just-yielding plum to my nose and inhale its sweet scent. It was heavenly … and strange. I looked around. People had carts. I take such experiences for granted now, but back then it was amazing to see people pushing large metal baskets on wheels and filling them with whatever produce they wanted. The store was crowded with shoppers grabbing bags and boxes, tossing them carelessly into their carts. They bought the freshest vegetables. They bought meat, all chopped, ground, and wrapped. I was used to seeing carcasses hanging whole in the souk, but in the supermarket even the chickens were neatly cut and packaged.

My love of cooking began when my family moved to San Francisco in the early '60s, when I was 16. My mother often worked late hours and would call on me, the eldest of four, to prepare dinner for the family. She would explain over the phone how to cook stews, soups and casseroles. "A little of this and a little of that," she would say. Her directions were easy to follow and always yielded tasty results. After five years of preparing excellent food like this, I decided that cooking was going to be my life. I started to collect recipes from newspaper food sections and all the well-known food magazines.

By the time I met my husband in 1965, my cooking repertoire had become impressive. Included were old family favorites such as Manti, Green Lentil Soup with Swiss Chard, and Layered Pasta with Cheese, recipes that had been passed down from my mother and grandmother, and all the innovations the contemporary culinary scene had to offer such as Moroccan salmon and rack of lamb. I discovered a program on television called "The French Chef" and became addicted. I never missed a show. This was my introduction to French cooking. I was fascinated with Julia Child because she made mistakes and was not afraid of them; she just went on like any other ordinary cook should. She made cooking fun.

In 1966, when my husband and I moved to Orange County, California, I was eager to experiment in the kitchen. We quickly made many friends and, as a new bride, I couldn't wait to begin entertaining. Staying home with my children gave me time to hone my skills. We hosted many parties in those days. The success of these gatherings gave me the confidence to start my own home catering business. It grew and grew, leading to the opening of my restaurant, Zov's Bistro.

Though it seemed natural, making the jump from home catering to the restaurant business was quite daunting. It happened like this: One day, while visiting a city in Orange County called Tustin, I found myself sipping a soda in an old ice cream parlor. For many months I had been looking for a place to house the bistro. As I looked around the shop, I noticed that the interior was in desperate need of a change. In fact, it was in

in horrid condition. I imagined redecorating the building into a fabulous, beautiful eatery. "Oh my goodness," I said to myself. "This is the place!"

The freeway was a mere block away—a perfect location. The place was not for rent, but I returned home and told my husband that I had just found the perfect site for my restaurant.

At first my husband thought I was crazy, and perhaps he was right. Opening a restaurant was risky; we would have to invest all of our savings. Then my mother came to town. For years I had worked with her at the grocery store that she and my father had owned in San Francisco. She knew my capabilities and convinced my husband saying, "You must let her do this. I know my daughter as well as I know my name. She will be able to do this. I've seen her do it. Don't worry. She is a good business woman."

How could he resist? My mother's contribution did not stop there. She mortgaged her home to aid in the restaurant's humble beginnings. Other family members helped as well. Zov's Bistro has been a family affair from the beginning.

Today, Zov's has grown from 1,500 to 12,000 square feet and employs 100. We serve 1,200 guests each day for breakfast, lunch and dinner. I arrive at the restaurant by 7 a.m., receive and make orders, greet vendors, review the specials of the day, create menus for special events, work with the kitchen staff, and design specialty menus.

Once a week, I drive to the local inner city high school where I teach about culinary arts, knowledge that will quality them for jobs when they graduate. Because cooking is my passion, I never consider it "work". This attitude is not lost on my restaurant team as we enjoy developing new recipes. This ensures the Zov's dining experience is an exceptional one for our guests.

Some customers have been dining with us for so long we feel like they are part of our family. That's because all of us—my husband, daughter, and son—work at the restaurant every day. We consider Zov's Bistro an extension of our home, and each patron is a friend coming over to dine. My cooking is a reflection of who I am—my family, heritage, travels, memories, and tastes. Each dish contains traces of my Mediterranean ancestry and my classical training.

I'm often asked, "What kind of food do you serve?" I'm still trying to find a suitable response. The recipes in this book draw upon my Middle Eastern heritage; however, you will find influences from around the globe—from regions where I've traveled including Vietnam, Italy, France, Spain, Japan, China and Mexico.

Each chapter of this book begins with a story from which you learn the inspiration behind each recipe. That's the thing about food and cooking—the stories that we remember.

I hope that the stories I offer in this book will give you a glimpse into why these recipes are special to me. As you recreate these dishes, and perhaps add your unique personal touch, I hope that you, too, will make your own special memories—memories that will last a lifetime!

ZOV'S PANTRY ESSENTIALS

High quality ingredients are always essential. They will really make a difference in your development as a cook. You'll be surprised, for instance, how much more vivid a salad dressing will taste using a high quality balsamic vinegar. I keep my own kitchen stocked with these premium basic ingredients and use them in almost every meal. Most of these ingredients can be found at most Middle Eastern Markets.

ALEPPO PEPPER

Aleppo is located in northern Syria. The ground red pepper from Aleppo is coarse like sand, dark red in color, and earthy. It has a nice bite to it. It is delicious served with soups, salads, and appetizers. The flavor of Aleppo pepper slowly develops in your mouth. It is predominantly used in Middle Eastern cuisine, although it has become mainstream. If Aleppo pepper is not available, substitute 4 parts of paprika to 1 part cayenne pepper. See mail order resource.

BALSAMIC VINEGAR

Authentic Balsamic vinegar is a radiant dark brown essence with an extraordinarily complex aroma. It is made from unfermented juice of Trebbiano grapes. Grape juice is aged in Balsamwood casks by the "Solera process" used in aging fine sherry wines. Specialty grocery stores carry this vinegar; including some Balsamics aged as long as 100 years.

BULGUR

For centuries, this has been the staple grain of Eastern Europe and the entire Middle East. In the Old Testament it was called "Arisah." It is basically whole wheat that has been washed and steamed, then hulled and either parched or dry cooled. It is then cracked and sifted into various sizes. It is widely used in Tabbouleh and pilafs. See mail order resource.

EXTRA-VIRGIN OLIVE OIL

Top-grade olives are used to make extra virgin olive oil. Its acidity is usually less than 1%, and it is a direct result of hand harvesting and cold pressing within 24 hours of harvest. Always try to purchase olive oil in smaller sizes, because air, heat, and light will cause the olive oil to turn rancid. Store at temperatures no higher than 55-58 F. I personally like to use either Greek or Italian olive oils but it is best to purchase what appeals to you most.

FETA CHEESE

Feta and Kasseri are among the oldest cheeses in the world. They are produced in most of the Middle Eastern and Eastern European countries. Feta cheese is classified in the soft cheese category. It can be made with either sheep's milk or cow's milk. I prefer the milder flavor of sheeps milk feta to the stronger aftertaste of goats milk feta. Feta is delicious served with fresh cucumbers, sliced tomatoes and mint, stuffed in warm pita bread for a mouth watering snack.

FRESHLY GROUND BLACK PEPPER

I love the flavor of roasted whole black peppercorns. When using roasted peppercorns you will get the full flavor of the pepper. The coarser the grind the less spicy it will be. The more finely it is ground, the spicier the flavor. White pepper comes from the heart of the black peppercorn and is hotter than ground black pepper.

KALAMATA OLIVES

An almond-shaped Greek olive that ranges in length from 1/2- to 1-inch, Kalamata olives are a dark eggplant color and have a flavor that can be rich and fruity. They are often slit to absorb the brine in which they are soaked.

KOSHER SALT

I always use kosher salt instead of "refined" salt when cooking. Kosher dissolves much more thoroughly and enhances the flavors of the recipe much more subtly than refined salt. When you can, use kosher salt.

LEMON PEPPER

I love using lemon pepper in my cooking; a very unique spice blend. It truly enhances the flavor of food.

POMEGRANATE MOLASSES

Pomegranate molasses comes in the form of thick syrup. It lends sweet and tart flavors to any dish. Concentrated pomegranate juice can be used as a substitute for pomegranate molasses, although it is slightly bitter. If using concentrated pomegranate juices, add a bit of sugar to balance the flavors. Both pomegranate molasses and concentrated pomegranate juice can be found at Middle Eastern markets, most specialty foods stores, and in the ethnic section of some supermarkets. See mail order resource.

SEASONED SALT

Equal amounts of dry spices consisting of ground black pepper, garlic powder, curry powder, cumin powder, chili powder, dry mustard, paprika, ground turmeric, ground thyme, and sugar are combined with salt. It is a wonderful combination that enhances the flavor of food.

SUMAC

Sumac is a shrub with dark red berries. It is native to the Eastern Mediterranean. It is highly esteemed for its distinct sour taste. Before the introduction of the lemon, the Egyptians and Romans used sumac as a sour element in food. Sumac is sold in a form of a powder and can be purchased in most ethnic food stores. See mail order resource.

TAHINI (SESAME SEED PASTE)

Tahini is another staple of Middle Eastern cooking, used mainly in sauces, dips, and salad dressings. Tahini is the essential ingredient in hummus and baba ganooj. It is made from hulled and ground sesame seeds. It has a nutty flavor and a creamy consistency. Tahini is very common nowadays and can be purchased at any natural foods stores, and in the ethnic foods section of most supermarkets.

YOGURT CHEESE

The history of yogurt goes back about 8,000 years. The creamy white cheese forms when the liquid has been drained from yogurt. It is all natural. Yogurt cheese takes on the flavor of whatever you mix it with. It can be magic, an ingredient that makes low- fat foods taste rich, creamy, and delicious. It can also be made with non-fat milk, drained of excess liquid until it is thick like sour cream. Yogurt cheese is also called lebni, meaning yogurt in Arabic. You will find it in specialty food stores and any Middle Eastern markets.

ZA-ATAR

A Middle Eastern spice blend that is a mixture containing ground sumac as a main ingredient, Za-atar contains marjoram, oregano, toasted sesame seeds, wild thyme and salt. It has a nutty and toasty flavor as well as lemony accent that comes from sumac. See "Sumac" above. See mail order resource.

CARDAMOM SEEDS

ALLSPICE

ZA-ATAR

WHOLE NUTMEG

CINNAMON STICK

WHOLE ALLSPICE

PAPRIKA

ZOV'S ESSENTIAL COOKING TECHNIQUES

The following are just a few guidelines that will yield authentic results as you practice these recipes. They are basic techniques most recipes rely on, but don't be afraid to experiment with them.

What distinguishes good cooking from great cooking is attention to detail. A touch of spice can make an ordinary tomato sauce extraordinary, even exotic. By adding dimensions of flavor, color, and texture, a few plump berries on a dessert elevates the experience of that dessert immeasurably. In fact, the very basic preparatory steps of every recipe offer opportunities for creating exceptional cooking.

Always use a sharp knife, and always tuck your fingers holding the food to keep them from getting nicked. For julienne or very small dice begin by slicing a vegetable very thinly lengthwise. To make julienne, stack several thin slices on top of each other, and slice them into matchsticks; to dice, gather the matchsticks together and chop them into equal pieces.

HOW TO TOAST NUTS

Toasting any type of nut (from pine nuts, walnuts, almonds or to pistachios) is simple. They add flavor as well as texture to the recipe. Spread the nuts on a baking sheet and bake in a 350-degree oven for about 5-6 minutes or until they are golden brown and fragrant. Watch carefully because nuts burn easily, especially pine nuts because they have a very high fat content. I recommend any leftover nuts be kept in a jar tightly covered and refrigerated. You may also freeze them indefinitely so they do not turn rancid.

HOW TO ROAST GARLIC

Preheat the oven to 350 degrees. Peel the outer layer of skin from the garlic head and leave the remaining skins intact. Cut off the pointed top portion with a small sharp, serrated knife, leaving the bulb intact but exposing the individual cloves of garlic. Place about 5 garlic heads, cut side up, in a small baking dish. Drizzle the garlic heads with 1/2 cup of olive oil. Bake, covered for 25-30 minutes, or until the cloves are soft when pressed. Cool completely. When ready to serve, use your fingers to squeeze the garlic cloves from the parchment-like covering.

HOW TO TOAST BLACK PEPPERCORNS

For the fullest flavor and aroma, place the whole peppercorns on a rimmed cookie sheet and bake in a 350-degree oven for 5-6 minutes, or until the oils emerge, causing them to crack. Cool before storing.

JULIENNE

MINCED

DICED

COARSELY CHOPPED

FINELY DICED

FINELY CHOPPED

MATCHSTICK

MEZZA

At our family gatherings it's not unusual to find from 10 to 30 Mezza—a delicious array of "small bites." At the table, they tease the senses so every guest becomes eager for the main course.

BEIRUT 1959

I remember the first time I tasted hummus and fell in love with it. We were in Beirut—the Paris of the Middle East. Beirut was the most glamorous, exciting city in the region, with skiing in winter, beautiful beaches in summer, ancient history, great shopping and a wild nightlife.

On our way to the United States my family and I stopped in Lebanon, arriving in Beirut at night. The city was ablaze with white and gold lights. We stayed at a local hotel, the Torig, popular because if its central location. From the lobby window, the streets around our hotel pulsed with life. Fashionable people crowded the wide sidewalks in front of cabarets across the street. Tangos and cha-chas were broadcast live from the cafés next door. Braided through the music and the noise of cars streaming along the avenue was the melodious laughter of the café patrons, their spirited conversations in French and Arabic.

The women wore lavish, mid-calf dresses and spiked, sling-back heels. In one hand they held a cigarette and in the other a short glass of ouzo, a bittersweet anise aperitif called "tiger's milk" because its vodka-clear texture turns milky white when poured over ice. The women chatted with ease while the men, clad in brand new suits, sat at tables smoking. They took turns sharing tall hookahs, with bulbous, blue glass bottoms and towering shafts of ornate silver. Their mood was as light as the smoke wafting from these pipes.

On every corner stood plain-looking Sudanese men wearing dark slacks and white shirts. They sold newspaper cones full of warm, roasted peanuts. It was the rich, roasted smell of peanuts that greeted me the next day when I went out with my family to explore the wonders of Beirut.

But we did not venture out before breakfast. Each morning of our stay there, our slender, wavy-haired waiter knocked enthusiastically on our door to retrieve our breakfast order, though each morning it was the same. A few moments later he would return with a tray full of satisfying treats: a pot of Earl Grey tea and a plate of feta cheese, black olives, and fresh mint. In the center of the tray was a bowl of hummus: gold-beige garbanzo beans pureed with a dash of cumin and a generous amount of tahini, ground sesame seed paste. Fresh lemon juice added a subtle tanginess to the dip, which was served in a terra cotta bowl and decorated with parsley, pickled red beets, and drizzled olive oil. Next to the hummus was a basket of pita bread, soft and steaming, fresh from a wood-burning stove.

The hummus we serve at Zov's Bistro comes as close to the spirit of Beirut as any I have ever tasted, and my guests tell us that Zov's is one of the best recipes. We add extra tahini in our hummus. Usually, the main ingredient of hummus is garbanzo beans—especially in American kitchens. Our recipe achieves a greater balance of flavor by adding more tahini, lemon juice and garlic. Then we carefully balance flavors and textures.

So when we encourage cooks to experiment with recipes, we want them to challenge their preconceptions of not only which ingredients go well together, but in what amounts. We invite them to consider flavor, texture, and presentation when weighing ingredients. As our version of hummus proves, even the simplest recipes offer opportunities for experimentation!

HUMMUS

IT SEEMS LIKE EVERYONE LOVES HUMMUS THESE DAYS AND EVERYONE MAKES IT DIFFERENTLY. THIS RECIPE IS EASY AND AUTHENTIC. IT'S DELICIOUS AS A DIP SERVED WITH TOASTED PITA WEDGES AND AS A SPREAD ON SANDWICHES. TRY IT IN ROASTED EGGPLANT OR GRILLED ZUCCHINI SANDWICHES!

1 garlic clove
2 cups freshly-cooked or canned
  garbanzo beans, drained
1/2 cup fresh lemon juice
1/2cup tahini paste (page 14)
1 1/2 teaspoons salt
1 teaspoon ground cumin
1/2 cup olive oil
2 teaspoons extra-virgin olive oil
  Paprika, for garnish
  Italian parsley sprigs, for garnish
  Toasted Pita Wedges (page 27)

Mince the garlic in a food processor. Add the garbanzo beans and lemon juice, and blend until creamy, scraping the sides of the bowl occasionally. Blend in the tahini, salt, and cumin. With the machine running, gradually add the olive oil through the feed tube and blend until the hummus is smooth and creamy, scraping the sides of the bowl occasionally.

Transfer the hummus to a serving bowl. Drizzle the extra-virgin olive oil over the hummus. Sprinkle with the paprika and garnish with the parsley sprigs. Serve with the toasted pita wedges

COOK'S NOTES: The hummus will keep for 2 days, covered and refrigerated

6 to 8 appetizer servings

WALNUT AND POMEGRANATE DIP

THE RICH NUTTY TEXTURE AND PERFECT BALANCE OF SWEET AND SOUR FLAVORS HAS MADE THIS HEALTHY DIP, ALSO KNOWN AS MUHAMMARA, VERY POPULAR, ESPECIALLY AMONG VEGETARIANS. IT'S WONDERFUL WITH BELGIAN ENDIVE SPEARS AND TOASTED PITA WEDGES (PAGE 27), AND WORKS WELL AS A SPREAD FOR SANDWICHES OR CRACKERS.

1 cup shelled walnuts, not toasted
2 small red bell peppers, seeded and
  coarsely chopped
1 small red onion, coarsely chopped
3 tablespoons fresh lemon juice
1/2 cup finely ground unseasoned dry breadcrumbs
1/4 cup pomegranate molasses (page 13)
2 tablespoons sugar
1 tablespoon ground cumin
2 1/2 teaspoons salt
1 teaspoon cayenne pepper
1/2 cup olive oil
1/4 cup pomegranate seeds, for garnish, optional
  Mint or Italian parsley sprigs, for garnish
3 heads Belgian endive, trimmed, leaves separated
  Toasted Pita Wedges (page 27)

Finely chop the walnuts in a food processor. Be careful not to grind them into a paste. They should be the texture of coarse breadcrumbs. Add the bell peppers, onion, and lemon juice. Pulse until the peppers are finely chopped. Add the breadcrumbs, pomegranate molasses, sugar, cumin, salt, and cayenne pepper. Using the pulse button, pulse once to blend. Gradually add the oil, blending just until the mixture resembles a very coarse puree.

Transfer the dip to a serving bowl. Garnish with the mint or parsley sprigs and serve with the Belgian endive leaves and toasted pita wedges.

COOK'S NOTES: The dip will keep for up to 3 days, covered and refrigerated. Sprinkle pomegranate seeds over the dip if they are available.

Makes about 3 cups

FIRE-ROASTED
EGGPLANT DIP

GRILLED EGGPLANT AND ROASTED GARLIC
LEND A WONDERFUL DEPTH OF FLAVOR
TO THIS TRADITIONAL BABA GHANOOJ.
IN AUTUMN, WHEN POMEGRANATES ARE
IN SEASON, GARNISH IT WITH POMEGRANATE
SEEDS. THE RUBY RED COLOR OF THE
POMEGRANATE SEEDS PROVIDES A DRAMATIC
COLOR CONTRAST AND TEXTURE. WHEN
POMEGRANATES ARE NOT IN SEASON, SIMPLY
GARNISH THE DIP WITH PAPRIKA AND FRESH
ITALIAN PARSLEY SPRIGS.

1 whole garlic head, unpeeled
7 tablespoons olive oil
2 eggplants (about 2 pounds total)
1/4 cup fresh lemon juice
1/4 cup tahini paste (page 14)
2 tablespoons plain yogurt
1 1/2 teaspoons salt
1 teaspoon ground cumin
1/2 teaspoon dried crushed red pepper
1/2 teaspoon ground black pepper
  Pomegranate seeds, for garnish
  Italian parsley sprigs, for garnish
  Toasted Pita Wedges, (page 24) lavash,
  or plain crackers

Preheat oven to 350°F. To roast the garlic, peel the
outer layer of skin from garlic head and leave remaining
skins intact. Cut off the pointed top portion with a
small sharp, serrated knife, leaving the bulb intact but
exposing individual cloves of garlic. Place the garlic
head, cut side up, in a small baking dish, and drizzle
garlic head with 2 tablespoon of olive oil. Bake,
covered, for 25-30 minutes or until cloves are soft
when pressed. Cool completely. When ready to serve,
use your fingers to squeeze the garlic cloves from
parchment-like covering.

Meanwhile, prepare a barbecue for medium-high heat.
Using a fork, pierce the eggplants on both sides several
times. Grill the eggplant until the skins are charred
and the centers are soft, turning them occasionally,
about 30 minutes total. Place the eggplants in a strainer
to drain and cool for 10 minutes. Cut the eggplants
lengthwise in half. Scraping as close to the eggplant
skins as possible, spoon the soft pulp into the strainer
set over a bowl. Discard the skins and any juices that
accumulate in the bowl.

In a food processor bowl, combine the eggplant pulp,
4 tablespoons of oil, the lemon juice, tahini, yogurt,
salt, cumin, crushed red pepper and black pepper.
Squeeze the garlic from the skins into the eggplant
mixture. Pulse just until a very coarse puree forms.
Transfer the eggplant dip to a serving bowl. Cover and
refrigerate until cold.

Just before serving, drizzle the remaining 1 tablespoon
of oil over the dip. Sprinkle with the pomegranate seeds
and garnish with the parsley sprigs. sprigs. Serve with
the pita bread wedges, lavash or crackers.

COOK'S NOTES: If you prefer a less smoky flavor, you can
roast the eggplants in the oven at 475°F until they are
charred on the outside and very tender inside, turning
them every 10 minutes, about 40 minutes total. The dip
will keep for 2 to 3 days, covered and refrigerated.

8 to 10 appetizer servings

YOGURT CHEESE SPREAD

THICK AND CREAMY YOGURT CHEESE, ALSO KNOWN AS LEBNI, IS AVAILABLE IN THE REFRIGERATED SECTION OF ETHNIC MARKETS. IT IS SOMEWHAT THICKER THAN CRÈME FRAÎCHE OR SOUR CREAM, AND THESE MAKE SUITABLE SUBSTITUTES. SEASONED WITH DRIED MINT, GARLIC, AND ALEPPO PEPPER, IT MAKES A VERY WONDERFUL CONDIMENT TO HAVE ON HAND AND MAY BE USED IN MANY WAYS THAT SOUR CREAM IS USED. I LOVE IT AS A DIP FOR FRESH VEGETABLES AND AS A SALAD DRESSING. I ALSO LIKE TO DOLLOP IT ATOP THE MANTI SOUP (PAGE 113). WHENEVER I'M NOT SURE ABOUT WHAT TO EAT FOR LUNCH, I SPREAD IT OVER FLAT PITA BREAD OR LAVASH, THEN TOP IT WITH SLICED CUCUMBERS, TOMATOES, AND MINT SPRIGS, AND ROLL IT UP LIKE A BURRITO.

8 ounces yogurt cheese (also labeled as lebni)
1 tablespoon dried mint
1 teaspoon garlic powder
3/4 teaspoon Aleppo pepper (page 12)
1/2 teaspoon salt
3 tablespoons olive oil
  Italian parsley sprigs, for garnish
  Mint sprigs, for garnish
  Warm pita bread wedges
  Aleppo pepper for garnish

Stir the yogurt cheese, dried mint, garlic powder, 3/4 teaspoon of Aleppo pepper, and salt in a medium bowl to blend. Transfer the mixture to a serving bowl. Drizzle it with the oil. Sprinkle with more Aleppo pepper. Garnish with parsley sprigs and mint sprigs. Serve with warm pita bread wedges.

COOK'S NOTES: This seasoned yogurt cheese spread will keep for 1 week. Just cover and refrigerate until ready to use.

Makes about 1 cup

TOASTED PITA WEDGES

THESE MIDDLE EASTERN "CHIPS" GO HAND-IN-HAND WITH THE HUMMUS (PAGE 24), FIRE-ROASTED EGGPLANT DIP (PAGE 26), AND THE WALNUT AND POMEGRANATE DIP (PAGE 24).

4 6-inch pita bread rounds, each cut into 8 wedges

Preheat the oven to 350°F. Arrange the pita wedges in a single layer on a large baking sheet. Bake until crisp and golden brown, about 7 minutes.

COOK'S NOTES: The pita chips can be made up to 2 days ahead. Cool and store them in a sealed plastic bag. Store chips at room temperature.

Makes about 2 1/2 dozen

EGGPLANT AND AVOCADO SALSA

GRILLED EGGPLANT LENDS ITS SMOKINESS
TO THE CREAMINESS OF AVOCADO IN THIS
DELIGHTFULLY UNUSUAL SALSA. ACTUALLY,
I INVENTED IT BY MISTAKE. I HAD INTENDED TO
MAKE BABA GANOOJ, AND AS I GATHERED ALL
THE INGREDIENTS FOR THE EGGPLANT DIP,
I DISCOVERED THAT I DIDN'T HAVE ANY TAHINI.
SO I PLAYED AROUND WITH THESE INGREDIENTS
(WHAT FUN!). THIS SALSA WAS BORN, AND IT'S
BEEN A HUGE HIT WITH MY FAMILY EVER SINCE.

2 large eggplants (about 2 pounds total)
2 red bell peppers
2 avocados, peeled, pitted and cubed
2 large plum tomatoes, diced
1/2 cup chopped fresh cilantro
1/2 cup chopped fresh Italian parsley
1/2 cup chopped fresh mint
1/3 cup fresh lemon juice
3 green onions, chopped
3 tablespoons olive oil
1 garlic clove, minced
1/2 teaspoon seasoned salt
1/2 teaspoon ground black pepper
1 1/2 teaspoons salt
  Lemon wedges, for garnish
  Toasted Pita Wedges (page 27) or crackers

Prepare a barbecue for medium-high heat. Using a small sharp knife, poke two 1-inch deep slits into each eggplant. Grill the eggplants until the skins are charred and the centers are soft, turning them occasionally, about 30 minutes total. Place the eggplant in a strainer and cool slightly. Cut the eggplants in half lengthwise in half and scoop out the pulp. Place the pulp in a strainer set over a bowl to drain any excess liquid. Cool the eggplant completely. Coarsely chop the eggplant and transfer it to a large bowl. Set aside.

Meanwhile, roast the red peppers on the barbecue or over a gas flame until lightly charred all over, about 10 minutes. Enclose the peppers in a plastic bag until cool enough to handle. Peel, seed, and dice the peppers. Add the diced peppers, avocados, tomatoes, cilantro, parsley, mint, lemon juice, green onions, olive oil, garlic, salt, black pepper, and seasoned salt. Add the eggplant. Gently toss to combine.

Transfer the salsa to serving bowls. Garnish with lemon wedges and serve with toasted pita wedges or crackers.

COOK'S NOTES: The eggplant may be cooked under the broiler instead of on the grill, if desired. To do so, line a baking sheet with foil or parchment paper. Place the eggplants on the prepared sheet and broil until the eggplants are very soft and the skin is charred, turning every 5 minutes, about 20 minutes total.

8 appetizer servings

GRILLED SHRIMP WITH MINT AND CILANTRO PESTO

BE SURE THE SHRIMP ARE NOT OVERCOOKED, AS THEIR TEXTURE WOULD BECOME STRINGY AND RUBBERY. COOKED JUST RIGHT, THEY ARE TENDER AND SUCCULENT. SHRIMP MAKE WONDERFUL FLAVOR TEMPLATES THAT REALLY ENHANCE THE TASTE OF THE DISH.

2 tablespoons olive oil
1 tablespoon chopped fresh Italian parsley
1 1/2 teaspoons minced garlic
1/2 teaspoon ground black pepper
1/4 teaspoon salt
24 jumbo shrimp, peeled, deveined, and tails still intact
2 tablespoons fresh lemon juice
1/2 cup Mint and Cilantro Pesto (recipe follows)
    Lemon wedges, for garnish
    Rosemary sprigs, for garnish

Stir the oil, parsley, garlic, pepper, and salt in a medium bowl to blend. Add the shrimp and toss to coat. Cover and refrigerate at least 15 minutes or up to 1 day.

Heat a grill pan over medium-high heat or prepare the barbecue for medium-high heat. Working in batches, grill the shrimp until they are pink and just opaque in the center, about 2 minutes per side. Place the cooked shrimp in a clean large bowl. Cool to room temperature, if desired. Toss the shrimp with the lemon juice and 2 tablespoons of the Mint and Cilantro Pesto just enough to coat. Spoon the remaining pesto into a small bowl.

Mound the shrimp on a platter. Garnish with lemon wedges and rosemary sprigs, and serve with the remaining pesto, passing toothpicks alongside.

COOK'S NOTES: These shrimp are also great atop salads and pasta. Try them with the Cannellini and Garbanzo Bean Salad with Oven-Roasted Tomatoes (page 69). Scallops, prawns, or lobster can be substituted for the shrimp.

8 to 12 appetizer servings

MINT AND CILANTRO PESTO

THIS DELICIOUS PESTO IS TERRIFIC WITH GRILLED SHRIMP. TRY IT ALSO WITH YOUR FAVORITE PASTA.

1/2 cup walnuts, toasted (page 18)
1/4 cup freshly grated Parmesan cheese
3 garlic cloves, peeled
1/2 teaspoon ground black pepper
1/2 teaspoon salt
1/4 teaspoon dried crushed red pepper
1 cup (packed) fresh cilantro leaves
1 cup (packed) fresh mint leaves
2 tablespoons fresh lemon juice
1/3 cup olive oil

Blend the nuts, cheese, garlic, black pepper, salt, and red pepper in a food processor until a thick paste forms. Add the cilantro, mint, and lemon juice. Blend until the cilantro and mint are finely chopped. With the machine running, gradually add the oil and blend until the mixture is smooth and creamy.

COOK'S NOTES: The pesto can be frozen for up to a month. Store it in an airtight container. Thaw it at room temperature before using.

Makes 1 cup

GRILLED EGGPLANT AND BAKED OLIVES WITH ROSEMARY AND THYME

THE ROBUST FLAVOR OF BAKED OLIVES WITH THE MEATY TEXTURE OF GRILLED EGGPLANT TEAM UP FOR A SUPERB SIDE DISH OR HEARTY APPETIZER. IT MAKES A FINE ADDITION TO AN ANTIPASTO PLATTER WITH SLICED BUFFALO MOZZARELLA CHEESE AND PROSCIUTTO. ALSO, THE BAKED OLIVES STAND ON THEIR OWN AS A CONDIMENT FOR GRILLED TOMATOES, OR A DIPPING SAUCE FOR FRENCH BREAD. OMITTING THE ANCHOVIES TURNS THIS INTO A VEGETARIAN SIDE DISH.

Baked Olives

2 cups Kalamata olives, pitted
1/4 cup fresh rosemary leaves
1/4 cup fresh thyme leaves
2 ounces oil-packed anchovies
1 tablespoon whole black peppercorns
2 whole garlic heads, unpeeled
1 1/2 cups extra virgin olive oil (see Cook's Note)

Grilled Eggplant

1/3 cup olive oil
2 tablespoons fresh lemon juice
2 tablespoons chopped fresh rosemary
2 tablespoons chopped fresh thyme
2 tablespoons minced garlic
2 teaspoons coarsely ground black pepper
1 teaspoon salt
2 eggplants (about 2 pounds),
   cut crosswise into 1/2-inch-thick rounds
4 ounces feta cheese, coarsely crumbled
2 large plum tomatoes, seeded and diced
   Basil or rosemary sprigs, for garnish

To make the baked olives: Preheat the oven to 350°F. Place the olives in an 8-inch-square baking dish. Sprinkle the rosemary and thyme leaves over the olives. Arrange the anchovies atop the herbs and drizzle any oil from the anchovies over. Sprinkle with the peppercorns. Cut the tops off the garlic heads so that the cloves are showing. Turn the heads upside-down and nestle them into the olive mixture. Pour enough olive oil over the olive mixture to almost cover the garlic completely.

Cover with foil and bake until the mixture bubbles and the garlic is very soft, about 45 minutes. Remove the garlic from the olive mixture and cool slightly. When garlic is cool enough to handle, squeeze the garlic cloves into a small bowl. Keep the olive mixture and garlic cloves warm.

Meanwhile, to make the grilled eggplant: Prepare the barbecue for medium-high heat. Whisk the oil, lemon juice, rosemary, thyme, garlic, pepper, and salt in a large bowl to blend. Arrange the eggplant slices on a baking sheet. Brush the oil mixture over both sides of the eggplant slices. Grill the eggplants until they are tender and grill marks appear, about 4 minutes per side.

Place 2 eggplant slices, overlapping slightly, in the center of each plate. Spoon 3 tablespoons of the olive mixture over the eggplant. Sprinkle the garlic cloves and feta cheese on top of the olive mixture, top with diced tomatoes. Garnish with basil or rosemary sprigs and serve.

COOK'S NOTES: The olive topping can be made up to 2 days ahead. Cover it and refrigerate. Serve at room temperature. Be sure to use a high-quality extra-virgin olive oil, as it marries well with the other robust flavors. If desired, instead of grilling the eggplant slices, bake them in a 400°F oven until they are tender and beginning to brown, about 20 minutes. Uncooked eggplant is quite bitter so be sure they are cooked all the way through.

This dish can also be served on a large platter for a buffet. To do so, just arrange the eggplant slices on the platter, overlapping slightly. Using a slotted spoon, spoon the olive mixture on top of the eggplant, then sprinkle with the garlic cloves, cheese and tomatoes. Garnish the platter with basil or rosemary sprigs. Any oil remaining from the olives can be served as a dipping sauce for bread.

8 to 10 servings

OLIVE SALAD WITH TAHINI

THIS SALAD IS VERSATILE AND MAKES A POPULAR PICNIC ITEM. USE IT AS A TOPPING FOR GRILLED CHICKEN OR SALMON. I LOVE IT STUFFED INTO A WARM PITA POCKET WITH SLICED GRILLED CHICKEN. DELICIOUS!

3 cups pitted extra-large green olives
1 large tomato, cored, seeded and finely diced
1 cup walnuts, toasted and coarsely chopped
2/3 cup finely chopped green onions
1/4 cup chopped fresh cilantro
1/4 cup chopped fresh Italian parsley
1/4 cup fresh lemon juice
2 garlic cloves, minced
1 jalapeño chili, seeded and minced
1 teaspoon Aleppo pepper (page 12)
1/2 cup Tahini Sauce (recipe follows)
  Teardrop tomatoes, for garnish

Soak the olives in a small bowl of hot water for 30 minutes (this will extract any excess saltiness from the olives). Drain the olives and pat them dry, then cut in half. Toss the olives, tomato, walnuts, green onions, cilantro, parsley, lemon juice, garlic, jalapeño chili, and Aleppo pepper in a large bowl. Pour the Tahini Sauce over the salad and toss again to coat.

Transfer the olive salad to a serving bowl. Garnish with teardrop tomatoes and serve.

COOK'S NOTES: The salad will keep up to 2 days, covered and refrigerated.

Serves 6 to 8

TAHINI SAUCE

THIS VERSATILE SAUCE COMPLIMENTS MANY RECIPES. TRY IT WITH THE SIMPLE POACHED SALMON (PAGE 216), OR ANY GRILLED FISH AND CHICKEN.

2 garlic cloves
1 cup tahini paste (page 14)
1/4 cup coarsely chopped fresh cilantro
1/4 cup coarsely chopped fresh Italian parsley
2 teaspoons salt
3/4 teaspoon ground black pepper
1/2 cup fresh lemon juice
1 cup (about) cold water

Finely chop the garlic in a food processor. Blend in the tahini, cilantro, parsley, salt, and pepper. With the machine running, add the lemon juice. Using a rubber spatula, scrape down the sides and bottom of the work bowl. Slowly blend in enough water to form a sauce with a consistency of buttermilk.

COOK'S NOTES: The sauce will keep up to 2 days. Store it in a glass jar with a tight-fitting lid and keep it refrigerated.

Makes about 2 1/2 cups

STUFFED GRAPE LEAVES WITH RICE AND HERBS

SERVED WITH TZATZIKI SAUCE (PAGE 182),
THESE GRAPE LEAVES ARE A FLAVORFUL, AND
HEALTHY APPETIZER. SINCE THEY CAN BE MADE
UP TO 4 DAYS AHEAD, ELIMINATING LAST MINUTE
PREPARATIONS, AND ARE AN IDEAL APPETIZER
FOR ENTERTAINING GUESTS.

3/4 cup olive oil
3 cups chopped onion
1 cup uncooked short-grain white rice
3 tablespoons tomato paste
4 cups water
3 tablespoons fresh lemon juice
2 tablespoons minced fresh parsley
1 1/2 teaspoons dried mint, crumbled
1 teaspoon dried dill
1 teaspoon lemon pepper or ground black pepper
1 teaspoon salt
2 large yellow onions, sliced
1 head Romaine lettuce
22 brined grape leaves from jar, rinsed,
   drained and patted dry
   Tzatziki Sauce (page 182)
   Lemon wedges

Heat the oil in a heavy large saucepan over medium-high heat. Add the chopped onion and saute until translucent, about 4 minutes. Stir in the rice and tomato paste. Add 2 cups of water and bring to a boil. Reduce heat to medium-low. Cover and simmer until the liquid is absorbed and the rice is almost tender, about 20 minutes. Stir in the lemon juice, parsley, mint, dill, lemon pepper or black pepper and salt. Cool completely.

Line the bottom of a large, deep skillet with the onion slices. Arrange half of the lettuce leaves over the onion slices. Place 1 grape leaf, smooth side down, on a clean kitchen towel. Trim the stem flush with the leaf. Spoon a generous tablespoon of the rice mixture onto the leaf, near the stem end. Roll up, folding the sides in and squeezing the roll as you go. The filling should be packed tightly in the leaf, and the roll will be about 3 1/2 inches long. Repeat with the remaining grape leaves and rice mixture. Arrange the stuffed grape leaves seam side down over the lettuce leaves in the skillet. Pour the remaining 2 cups of water over the stuffed grape leaves. Cover with the remaining lettuce leaves. Bring to a boil over high heat. Reduce the heat to medium-low. Cover and simmer for 1 hour.

Cool slightly (do not uncover). Transfer the skillet to the refrigerator and cool completely. To prevent discoloration, do not remove the lid from the pan or touch the grape leaves until after they are cold.

Discard the lettuce from atop the stuffed grape leaves. Arrange the stuffed grape leaves on a platter. Serve cold with the Tzatziki Sauce and lemon wedges.

COOK'S NOTES: The stuffed grape leaves can be made up to 4 days ahead. Keep them covered and refrigerated.

For interesting flavor variations, add 1/2 cup of pine nuts or 3 tablespoons of currants to the rice mixture when you add the herbs.

Makes 22

SAN FRANCISCO 1961

Some afternoons in San Francisco, I would return
from high school to find my mother preparing pickles.
On those days, the moment I came home I knew
I would not leave again soon. I wouldn't want to!
The warm, exotic aroma of curry and pickling spices
would keep me in the kitchen with mother. I'd have
to search for her among bowls full of colorful, whole
vegetables: hot-sweet jalapeños, baby bright-green
cabbages, purple-ridged turnips. I'd have to sift through
jars of dill needles, grainy salt, whole peppercorns,
minced garlic. I'd find her slightly bent over the
kitchen sink, steam rising up, as she sterilized Bell
jars for storing the pickles.

On the small TV on the counter," I Love Lucy " aired
as Mother and I chatted about school and friends.
Her hands deftly worked the cabbage, pulling off each
leaf and blanching them until they were softish, but
still had their crunch. She'd separate the cauliflower
flowers and mix them with the cabbage and baby
cucumbers. She'd add salt and bay leaves to the mix
of vinegar, water, dill, peppercorn and curry. The air
we breathed became thicker and thicker with the
fragrance of spices.

Rows of pickled jars still line my mother's cupboards.
She keeps extra jars of pickled cabbage, my favorite;
it retains its slight crunchiness while taking on the
curry's flavor and it's beautiful amber color.

ASSORTED PICKLED VEGETABLES

THE CUCUMBER USED IN THIS RECIPE IS THE THIN ARMENIAN CUCUMBER, SOMETIMES CALLED JAPANESE CUCUMBER. IT IS VERY CRISP, WITH MELON-LIKE LENGTHWISE RIDGES. IN THIS VERSION, CUCUMBERS ARE TEAMED WITH CAULIFLOWER, CABBAGE, CARROTS AND CELERY. BUT AT OUR HOUSE, WHOLE JARS OF CUCUMBER-ONLY OR CABBAGE-ONLY WERE VERY POPULAR.

1 head cauliflower (about 2 pounds),
  cut into small florets
1/2 head green cabbage (about 12 ounces),
  cut into 6 wedges
6 pickling cucumbers, each cut lengthwise into 6 spears
6 carrots, peeled, cut into sticks
6 celery stalks, cut into sticks
6 ounces thin green beans, ends trimmed
18 small chile peppers (such as green and red jalapeño
  chilies, and yellow chilies), halved lengthwise but still
  attached at the stem end
18 garlic cloves, peeled
9 cups water
3 cups distilled white vinegar
3/4 cup kosher salt (page 13)
3 tablespoons pickling spice
4 teaspoons dried pearl barley
1 teaspoon curry powder

Dividing equally, arrange the vegetables, chilies, and garlic cloves decoratively in six 1-quart jars.

Stir the water, vinegar, salt, pickling spice, pearl barley, and curry powder in a large saucepan over medium-low heat just until the salt dissolves. Pour the brine over the vegetables to cover completely. Cover the jars tightly with their lids. Store the pickled vegetables at room temperature for 1 week. Since the vegetables will shrink as they pickle, you can add more vegetables to the jar at this point. Refrigerate the pickled vegetables until cold, at least 8 hours or up to 1 month.

COOK'S NOTES: You can add almost any type of vegetable. I like crunchy vegetables such as carrots and cauliflower. However, omit using beets, as they will turn all the other vegetables red. You can add other spicy peppers as well. I like jalapeño, serrano chilies, or even the long Anaheim chilies. Do not use bell peppers.

Yields six 1-quart jars

SAVORY BEEF BRIOUATS

A BRIOUAT IS A NORTH AFRICAN PASTRY
FILLED WITH VARIOUS SWEETS OR MEATS.
I FIRST TRIED THIS MEAT-FILLED PASTRY
IN MOROCCO AND WAS IMPRESSED BY THE
LIGHT CRUNCHINESS OF THE DOUGH AND
THE SPICINESS OF THE BEEF. I ADDED NUTS
TO GIVE THE FILLING AN EXTRA DIMENSION OF
TEXTURE. I ALSO RECOMMEND EXPERIMENTING
WITH THE FILLING. THE ADDITION OF ASSORTED
WILD MUSHROOMS, FOR INSTANCE, WOULD
SURELY ENHANCE THE MULTI-LAYERED FLAVORS
OF THIS FABULOUS APPETIZER.

14 sheets frozen phyllo dough, (see cook's notes)
1 1/2 tablespoons vegetable oil
8 ounces ground beef (7% fat)
1 cup finely chopped onion
2 tablespoons chilled butter, cut into small pieces
1/4 teaspoon ground allspice
1/4 teaspoon ground cinnamon
1/4 teaspoon ground cumin
1/4 teaspoon ground black pepper
1/4 teaspoon salt
1/8 teaspoon ground cloves
1/16 teaspoon dried crushed red pepper
1/2 cup cooked long-grain white rice
1/4 cup currants, dark raisins, or golden raisins
1/4 cup pine nuts, toasted (page 18)
2 tablespoons pistachios, toasted and chopped
2 tablespoons slivered almonds, toasted and chopped
2 tablespoons coarsely chopped cilantro leaves
2 tablespoons freshly chopped chives
1 tablespoon coarsely chopped Italian parsley
1/2 cup (1 stick) unsalted butter, melted

Allow the box of phyllo dough to stand at room
temperature for 30 minutes. (This makes the sheets
much easier to separate).

Heat the oil in a large nonstick skillet over medium-
high heat. Add the beef and onion, and cook until the
meat is dark brown and the onions are caramelized
to a rich brown color, breaking up the meat with a
wooden spoon so that no visible clumps remain, about
15 minutes. Lower the heat to low. Stir in the chilled
butter, allspice, cinnamon, cumin, black pepper, salt,
cloves, and red pepper. Then add the cooked rice,
currants, pine nuts, pistachios, and almonds. Remove
from the heat and mix in the cilantro, chives, and
parsley. Cool completely. The beef mixture can be made
up to this point 1 day ahead covered and stored in the
refrigerator until ready to use.

Preheat the oven to 350°F. Line 2 heavy large baking
sheets with parchment paper. Unroll the phyllo sheets
on a dry flat surface. Carefully remove 1 sheet of
phyllo and lay it on a work surface. (Keeping the
remaining phyllo covered with plastic wrap and a damp
kitchen towel). Brush the phyllo sheet with some
melted butter. Top with a second sheet of phyllo, and
brush it with some melted butter. Cut the layered
sheets crosswise, into four, 4-inch-wide strips. Spoon
1 generous tablespoon of beef filling in a narrow strip
along the edge nearest to you, then roll up the filling
tightly with the phyllo, folding the sides in and
forming a cigar. Transfer the cigars to the prepared
baking sheets, seam side down, and brush the tops with
more melted butter. Repeat with the remaining phyllo
sheets, melted butter, and beef mixture, forming
28 cigars total.

Bake the pastries until they are golden brown, about
18-25 minutes. Cool slightly. Arrange the pastries on a
platter and serve warm.

COOK'S NOTES: Thaw the phyllo dough in the
refrigerator for up to 24 hours before you use it. Any
remaining sheets of phyllo can be refrozen. In fact,
you can make the briouats a month ahead of time and
freeze them. Be sure to bake them frozen.

Makes 28 pastries

SAUTÉED CALAMARI WITH TOMATOES AND OREGANO

WHEN I ENTERTAIN AT HOME, I LOVE TO OFFER THIS EASY APPETIZER. TOSSING THE CRISP CALAMARI IN A DELICIOUS WHITE WINE SAUCE AND SPOONING IT OVER CROSTINI REALLY MAKES IT IMPRESSIVELY UNIQUE, A DELICIOUS ALTERNATIVE TO ORDINARY DEEP-FRIED CALAMARI.

12 1/3-inch-thick baguette slices
1 tablespoon plus 1/4 cup olive oil
6 ounces cleaned calamari bodies,
  cut crosswise into 1/4-inch-thick rings
1/2 cup (about) rice flour
1 1/2 tablespoons minced garlic
1 cup seeded diced tomatoes
2 tablespoons chopped fresh oregano
1/2 cup dry white wine
1/4 cup whipping cream
1 tablespoon fresh lemon juice
1 teaspoon ground black pepper
1/2 teaspoon salt
6 tablespoons (3/4 stick) unsalted butter,
  cut into small pieces
  Oregano sprigs, for garnish

Preheat the oven to 375°F. Place the baguette slices in a single layer on a baking sheet. Lightly brush the baguette slices with 1 tablespoon of oil. Bake until the baguette slices are golden, about 8 minutes. Arrange the crostini side by side on a platter

Dredge the calamari rings in the rice flour to coat lightly, shaking off the excess flour. Set aside. Heat the remaining 1/4 cup of oil in a heavy large skillet over medium-high heat. Add the garlic and sauté until pale golden, 30 seconds. Immediately add the calamari, and saute until pale golden, about 1 minute. Using a slotted spoon, transfer the calamari to a large bowl. Increase the heat to high. Add the tomatoes and chopped oregano to the skillet and sauté just until the tomatoes are heated through, about 30 seconds. Add the wine and cream. Boil until the sauce thickens slightly, about 2 minutes. Stir in the lemon juice, salt and pepper. Reduce the heat to low and whisk in the butter 1 piece at a time. Pour the sauce over the calamari and toss to coat.

Spoon the calamari mixture over the crostini. Garnish with the oregano sprigs and serve immediately.

COOK'S NOTES: Use the freshest calamari you can find to make the most of the different textures and flavors this dish offers.

The crostini can be made 2 days ahead. Store them in an airtight container or plastic bag and keep them at room temperature. When ready to serve, just arrange them on a platter before you begin preparing the calamari mixture to spoon over them.

Serves 6 to 12

CRAB AND SHRIMP PHYLLO TRIANGLES

UNTIL RECENTLY, I USED THIS WONDERFUL RECIPE SOLELY FOR CRAB DIP. ONE DAY, THOUGH, I FOUND MYSELF WITH A BUNCH OF PHYLLO DOUGH LEFTOVER FROM A PARTY. IT OCCURRED TO ME TO WRAP THE DIP INTO THE PHYLLO AND THIS GREAT TWIST ON A STAPLE PARTY APPETIZER WAS BORN.

14 sheets frozen phyllo dough, thawed
4 ounces cream cheese, room temperature
1/2 cup finely chopped red onion
4 green onions, finely chopped
2 tablespoons chopped fresh dill
2 tablespoons finely chopped fresh Italian parsley
1 tablespoon finely chopped fresh chives
2 tablespoons fresh lemon juice
2 tablespoons prepared horseradish
1/2 teaspoon salt
1/4 teaspoon ground black pepper
8 ounces fresh crabmeat, picked over
4 ounces cooked bay shrimp
1/2 cup chopped fresh uncooked spinach
1/2 cup (1 stick) unsalted butter, melted

Allow the box of phyllo dough to stand at room temperature for 30 minutes. (The sheets are much easier to separate when they are at room temperature).

Stir the cream cheese, red onion, green onions, dill, parsley, chives, lemon juice, horseradish, salt, and pepper in a large bowl. Mix in the crabmeat, shrimp, and spinach. The crab mixture will resemble a nice, thick crab salad. Set aside.

Preheat the oven to 350°F. Line 2 heavy large baking sheets with parchment paper. Unroll the phyllo sheets on a dry flat surface. Carefully remove 1 sheet of phyllo and lay it on a work surface (keep the remaining phyllo covered with plastic wrap and a damp kitchen towel). Brush the phyllo sheet with some melted butter. Top with a second sheet of phyllo, and brush with some melted butter. Cut the layered sheets lengthwise, into four 3-inch-wide strips. Place 1 generous tablespoon of the crab mixture on the bottom right hand corner of each strip of layered phyllo. Working with one layered phyllo strip at a time, fold 1 corner of phyllo over the crab mixture, forming a small triangle. Repeat folding the phyllo triangle up and over onto itself as you would fold a flag, brushing the edge of the last fold with more butter to seal. Transfer the triangles to the prepared baking sheets, seam side down, and brush the tops with more melted butter. Repeat with the remaining phyllo sheets, melted butter, and crab mixture, forming 28 triangles total.

Bake the pastries until they are golden brown, about 18- 25 minutes. Cool slightly. Arrange the pastries on a platter and serve warm.

COOK'S NOTE: The crab mixture, served warm, makes a fabulous dip. To serve the crab mixture as a dip, just spoon it into a crock and bake it at 350°F until it bubbles around the sides and is heated through, about 25 minutes. Serve it with crostini, lavash crackers, or thin slices of French baguettes.

You can make these triangles ahead of time, and freeze them until needed. As with the other phyllo appetizers, be sure to bake them frozen.

If you are substituting dried herbs, use less than half the amount that is called for in the recipe. Dried herbs yield much stronger flavors.

Makes 28 pastries

CHEESE AND PARSLEY
PHYLLO TRIANGLES

PHYLLO DOUGH COMES FRESH OR FROZEN
IN 1-POUND BOXES WITH ABOUT 26 TO 30 VERY
THIN SHEETS. I LOVE WORKING WITH PHYLLO.
IT IS AN ALTERNATIVE TO PUFF PASTRY AND
OTHER BUTTERY DOUGHS. IT'S EASY TO WORK
WITH, AND THE RESULTS ARE DELICIOUS
AND COMFORTING.

12 sheets frozen phyllo dough, thawed (see cook's note)
6 ounces feta cheese, crumbled (about 1 1/2 cups)
3 ounces fontina cheese, shredded (about 1 cup)
2 ounces Monterey Jack cheese,
  shredded (about 3/4 cup)
1/2 cup chopped fresh Italian parsley
2 large eggs, beaten to blend
1 tablespoon minced shallot
1/2 cup (1 stick) unsalted butter, melted

Allow the box of phyllo dough to stand at room temperature for 30 minutes (the sheets are much easier to separate when they are room temperature). Mix the feta, fontina, and Monterey Jack cheeses in a medium bowl to blend. Stir in the parsley, eggs, and shallot. Set the filling aside.

Preheat the oven to 350°F. Line 2 heavy large baking sheets with parchment paper. Unroll the phyllo sheets on a dry flat surface. Carefully remove 1 sheet of phyllo and lay it on a work surface (keep the remaining phyllo covered with plastic wrap and a damp kitchen towel). Brush the phyllo sheet with some melted butter. Top with a second sheet of phyllo, and brush it with some melted butter. Cut the layered sheets lengthwise, into four 3-inch-wide strips. Place 1 generous tablespoon of filling on the bottom right hand corner of each strip of layered phyllo. Working with one layered phyllo strip at a time, fold 1 corner of phyllo over the filling, forming a small triangle (see page 47). Repeat folding the phyllo triangle up and over onto itself as you would fold a flag, brushing the edge of the last fold with more butter to seal. Transfer the triangles to the prepared baking sheets, seam side down, and brush the tops with more melted butter. Repeat with the remaining phyllo sheets, melted butter, and filling, forming 24 triangles total.

Bake the pastries until they are golden brown, about 18-25 minutes. Cool slightly. Arrange the pastries on a platter and serve warm.

COOK'S NOTES: Thaw the phyllo dough in the refrigerator for up to 24 hours before you use it. Any remaining sheets of phyllo can be refrozen. These triangles make a fabulous accompaniment to salads! I recommend freezing some of the unbaked pastries so that you have them available to serve at luncheons. Store them airtight in the freezer for up to 2 weeks. You do not need to thaw the frozen pastries before baking them.

Makes 24

SALADS

I have perfected my favorite traditional salads throughout my career. They are chosen for their rich textures and colors, divine taste, and ease of preparation. How wonderful for the busy cook.

NICE, FRANCE 1998

An outstanding salad begins with the freshest ingredients and nothing beats a Farmers' Market for providing not only fresh produce, but a wealth of sensual experience.

Some years ago, I was guest chef on a luxury cruise ship. We stopped for a few days in the south of France. It was early summer and the weather was divine: soft ocean breezes cooled uninterrupted, butter-yellow sunlight. One morning I took a stroll and followed the breeze. It led me down a brick street lined with tall stone buildings that opened up into a small square. Rows and rows of striped, bright-colored awnings had transformed the square into a sea of color—the Farmers' Market! People meandered from stall to stall, large baskets in their arms, batons of bread leaning on their shoulders.

Although it was still early morning, the market was already loud and lively; everyone was laughing, singing, and chattering in French. I explored the clean aisles, admiring the amazing French produce. At one stand, a small woman in a bright red hat and dark sunglasses caught my eye. At first I thought she was angry with me; her voice sharp, she shook her head as if to say "no" as she spoke. Soon I realized I was misinterpreting her body language altogether. She wasn't remonstrating me, in fact, it was quite the opposite…she was passionate about the spices and herbs that filled her wooden boxes and she transcended the language barrier to share her enthusiasm for the deeply musky mixture of lavender, rosemary and thyme she displayed. This encounter only spurred my imagination into daydreams of cooking.

Next door, a man sold grains and beans: lentils, wild rice, black beans, red beans, white beans, and green beans in lovely long strands. The presentation of these dry goods amazed me. A colorful, zigzag-cut label stuck out of each heap, naming the goods and their price. In front of the staples were square boxes wrapped in beautiful, paisley-patterned cloth and filled with aromatic dry mint leaves, lavender, rosemary, dry anise, rose buds, parsley and oregano.

Further down, men in crisp white aprons made ham and cheese croissant sandwiches. Rotisserie chickens roasted on spits, and stands offered warm Brie oozing from under its soft white skin. The aromas were intoxicating even in the open air, but the yeasty warmth of fresh- baked bread nearly drove me wild. "Try some," the vendors enticed, slicing the cheese and spreading it over bread slivers or slices of pear, translucent with juice.

As I strolled up and down the picturesque aisles of the farmers' market, I was astonished by the beauty and bounty displayed by the vendors. The market was like nothing I had ever seen before. Each basket of fruit, each flat of vegetables was arranged so artistically, the food seemed exotic, even priceless. Little white baskets of cherry tomatoes gleamed jewel-like in neat, exact rows. Handled boxes held blackberries so thick with juice one could taste, on sight, their warm sweetness. Violet-blue plums in clear tubs formed peaked hills of succulence. Even the radishes had been arranged perfectly, bundled tightly into red and white-bulbed bouquets, their frothy greens bursting on top. The table was a tiered, red and green striped living canvas.

Isn't this what a great salad really is: a living work of art? The background is comprised of greens—baby mesclun, butter lettuce, red-leaved lettuce—and the link is extra-virgin olive oil. Toss in a few drops of fresh-squeezed lemon juice or a dash of red wine vinegar. Gently toss the greens with mint, chives, and oregano. To finish add whatever your imagination desires: plump green olives, sweet slivers of yellow and red peppers, earthy mushrooms, and juicy summer tomatoes. And on the side: pear slices slathered in warm French Brie!

MIXED BABY GREENS WITH AIR-DRIED BEEF AND SHERRY VINAIGRETTE

BASTERMA IS A POPULAR AIR-DRIED BEEF TRADITIONALLY EATEN IN THE MIDDLE EAST FOR BREAKFAST WITH SCRAMBLED EGGS, OR ON A SANDWICH. I'VE ADAPTED IT HERE AS A SALAD BECAUSE IT COMPLIMENTS THE FLAVORS OF THE SHERRY VINAIGRETTE AND THE TEXTURE OF ARUGULA SO COMPLETELY. I DO RECOMMEND THE BEEF AS A SIDE TO SCRAMBLED EGGS THOUGH (IT'S DELICIOUS!). STORE ANY LEFTOVER BALSAMIC SYRUP IN A GLASS JAR WITH A TIGHT FITTING LID. IT'S ALSO DELICIOUS DRIZZLED OVER STRAWBERRIES OR ICE CREAM

Balsamic Syrup
1 cup balsamic vinegar

Sherry Vinaigrette
1/3 cup sherry vinegar
3 tablespoons minced shallots
1 teaspoon salt
1/2 teaspoon ground black pepper
1/2 cup hazelnut oil or olive oil

Salad
5 ounces arugula (about 8 cups)
1 small head radicchio, torn into bite-size pieces
1 head frisée or curly endive, torn into bite-size pieces
1 small red onion, cut into paper-thin slices
1 green apple, unpeeled, cored and
  cut into paper-thin slices
1 cup toasted walnuts, coarsely chopped (page 18)
  Parmesan cheese, for garnish
18 thin slices basterma (air-dried beef)
1 red apple, unpeeled, cored and
  cut into paper-thin slices

To make the balsamic syrup: Bring the balsamic vinegar to a boil in a heavy small saucepan over medium heat. Reduce the heat to low and simmer until the vinegar is reduced by half and syrupy, stirring occasionally, about 15 minutes. Cool completely.

Meanwhile, to make the vinaigrette: Whisk the Sherry vinegar, shallots, salt, and pepper in a large bowl. Gradually whisk in the oil to blend.

To make the salad: In a large bowl, toss the arugula, radicchio, frisée, onion, green apple, and walnuts with enough vinaigrette to coat. Season to taste with salt and pepper.

Mound the salad in the center of each plate. Drizzle the balsamic syrup around each salad. Shave some Parmesan cheese over the salads. Then top each with 3 slices of basterma. Garnish with the red apple slices and serve.

COOK'S NOTES: Basterma is available at most Middle Eastern markets. Ask the butcher to slice it as thin as possible. If you're not able to find basterma, you can substitute prosciutto ham, which is available at Italian markets, most specialty foods stores, and some supermarkets.

Serves 6 to 8

TRADITIONAL TABBOULEH SALAD

A TRUE TABBOULEH USES A VERY SMALL AMOUNT OF BULGUR AND CONSISTS MOSTLY OF CHOPPED FRESH PARSLEY AND VEGETABLES. IN THE MIDDLE EAST, IT'S OFTEN SPOONED DOWN THE CENTER OF A ROMAINE LETTUCE LEAF AND ROLLED UP LIKE A CIGAR. SERVED IN A BOWL WITH THE LETTUCE LEAVES ON THE SIDE MAKES IT VERY EASY TO PUT TOGETHER. I ALSO LIKE TO SPOON THE TABBOULEH ATOP ENDIVE LEAVES OR SMALL HEARTS OF ROMAINE LETTUCE LEAVES AND ARRANGE THEM ON A PLATTER TO SERVE AS HORS D'OEUVRES. FOR VARIETY, YOU CAN TOP THE SALAD WITH GRILLED FISH, SHELLFISH, OR CHICKEN AND SERVE IT AS AN ENTRÉE.

2 tablespoons fine bulgur (#1 grade) (page 12)
5 plum tomatoes, seeded, and finely diced
2 cucumbers, peeled, seeded, and finely diced
2 1/2 cups chopped fresh Italian parsley
   (about 2 bunches)
2/3 cup finely chopped green onions
1/2 cup chopped fresh mint
1/2 cup finely diced red onion
1/2 cup extra-virgin olive oil
1/3 cup fresh lemon juice
1 teaspoon ground black pepper
1 teaspoon salt
1 teaspoon seasoned salt (see page 13)
1/2 teaspoon lemon pepper
   Red leaf lettuce or romaine lettuce leaves,
   Lemon slices, for garnish

Place the bulgur in a large bowl. Spoon the tomatoes directly over the bulgur. Spoon the cucumbers, then the parsley, green onions, mint and red onion atop the salad. Whisk the oil, lemon juice, black pepper, salt, seasoned salt, and lemon pepper in a small bowl to blend. Pour the dressing over the salad and toss to coat.

Line a large bowl with the lettuce leaves. Spoon the tabbouleh into the bowl and serve.

COOK'S NOTES: Be sure to layer the tomatoes directly over the bulgur so that the bulgur can absorb the tomato juices. By doing this, you do not need to soak the bulgur to soften it. You can prepare all of the chopped ingredients a day ahead, adding the dressing just before serving.

The secret to making a tasty tabbouleh is balancing the flavors of the lemon juice with the salt (neither should dominate). A high-quality extra-virgin olive oil is essential.

Serves 6 to 8

FATTOUCH SALAD WITH PURSLANE AND SUMAC VINAIGRETTE

PURSLANE HAS BEEN WIDELY USED IN THE MIDDLE EAST AND MEXICO (WHERE IT IS KNOWN AS VERDULAGUS). THE LOW-GROWING SUCCULENT PLANT WITH REDDISH STEMS HAS A MILD LEMONY TASTE AND CRISP TEXTURE. IT IS EXTREMELY RICH IN OMEGA-3 FATTY ACIDS AND ANTIOXIDANTS, TWO COMPONENTS PROVEN TO REDUCE YOUR CHANCES OF DEVELOPING HEART DISEASE AND STOMACH DISORDERS, AMONG OTHER AILMENTS. ALTHOUGH SOMETIMES DIFFICULT TO FIND, LOOK FOR PURSLANE IN LATIN AMERICAN MARKETS, FARMER'S MARKETS, AND SOME SPECIALTY FOOD STORES. IF NOT AVAILABLE USE ALL ROMAINE LETTUCE FOR THIS SALAD.

Sumac Vinaigrette
1/3 cup fresh lemon juice
1 garlic clove, minced
1 teaspoon ground black pepper
1 teaspoon ground sumac, optional (page 13)
1 teaspoon salt
1/3 cup olive oil

Salad
2 cups thinly sliced romaine lettuce
2 cups purslane leaves (leaves only)
3 large ripe tomatoes cut into large chunks
2 medium cucumbers, peeled, seeded and
  sliced diagonally
1 large red onion, thinly sliced
1 large green bell pepper, seeded and
  cut into matchstick-size strips
1 large red bell pepper, seeded and
cut into matchstick-size strips
1 large yellow pepper, seeded and
  cut into matchstick-size strips
1 bunch fresh mint, leaves coarsely
  chopped (about 1 1/2 cups)
4 green onions, thinly sliced diagonally
  Salt and ground black pepper, to taste
2 pita breads, split, toasted

To make the sumac vinaigrette: Whisk the lemon juice, garlic, black pepper, sumac, and salt, in a large bowl to blend. Gradually whisk in the oil. Set the vinaigrette aside.

To make the salad: Combine the lettuce, purslane leaves, tomatoes, cucumbers, red onion, bell peppers, mint, and green onions in a large bowl. Toss the salad with enough vinaigrette to coat. Season the salad to taste with salt and pepper to taste. Mound the salad in wide serving bowls or plates. Coarsely crumble the pita bread over the salads and serve immediately.

COOK'S NOTE: This salad compliments grilled chicken, fish or beef, deliciously. You can prepare the vinaigrette up 2 days ahead, cover the vinaigrette in a tight fitting glass jar and refrigerate it.

Serves 6 to 8

ORZO SALAD WITH SUN-DRIED TOMATOES AND KALAMATA OLIVES

MANY PEOPLE MISTAKE ORZO FOR RICE, BUT IT'S REALLY AN ITALIAN PASTA. ITS LARGE, SOFT "GRAINS" TRANSFORM OTHERWISE SIDE-DISH-ONLY RECIPES INTO HEARTY MAIN COURSES. THIS SALAD ALSO MAKES A SPLENDID SIDE DISH. FOR INSTANCE, A SUMMER PICNIC PAIRING THE SIMPLE POACHED SALMON (PAGE 216) AND THIS SALAD WOULD BE DELICIOUS!

Vinaigrette

1/4 cup fresh lemon juice
1 tablespoon minced shallot
1 tablespoon white wine vinegar
2 teaspoons Dijon mustard
1 teaspoon ground black pepper
1 teaspoon salt
1/4 teaspoon dried crushed red pepper
1/2 cup olive oil

Salad

1 teaspoon salt, plus more to taste
1 pound asparagus, trimmed and
  cut diagonally into 2-inch pieces
1 pound orzo pasta
4 tablespoons olive oil
8 ounces cremini, portobello, or
  stemmed shiitake mushrooms, sliced
3 tablespoons chopped shallots
2 tablespoons minced garlic
1 cup sun-dried tomatoes packed in oil, drained and
  cut to matchstick-size strips
1 small red bell pepper, seeded and thinly sliced
1 small red onion, thinly sliced
6 green onions, thinly sliced
6 ounces feta cheese, coarsely crumbled
1/2 cup coarsely chopped fresh mint
1/2 cup freshly grated Parmesan cheese
1/2 cup pitted Kalamata olives, sliced or halved
1/2 cup thinly sliced fresh basil
1 cup pine nuts, toasted (page 18)
  Teardrop tomatoes, for garnish
  Italian parsley leaves, for garnish

To make the vinaigrette: Whisk the lemon juice, shallot, vinegar, mustard, black pepper, salt and crushed red pepper in a large bowl to blend. Gradually whisk in the oil. Set the vinaigrette aside.

To make the salad: Combine 4 quarts of water and 1 teaspoon of salt in a large pot. Bring the water to a boil over high heat. Add the asparagus and cook just until it turns bright green, about 30 seconds. Immediately transfer the asparagus to a large bowl of ice water (reserve the boiling salted water). Let the asparagus stand until cold. Drain the asparagus and pat completely dry.

Meanwhile, return the salted water to a boil. Add the orzo and cook until it is tender but still firm to the bite, stirring occasionally, about 8 minutes. Drain the orzo and transfer it to a large bowl. (Be certain not to rinse it or you'll wash out its nutrients and starches.) Toss the orzo with 2 tablespoons of oil. Cool the orzo to room temperature.

Heat the remaining 2 tablespoons of oil in a heavy large skillet over medium-high heat. Add the mushrooms and sauté for 2 minutes. Reduce the heat to medium. Add the shallots and garlic, and sauté until the liquid from the mushrooms evaporates and the mixture is golden brown, about 5 minutes. Combine the mixture with the orzo.

Add the asparagus, sun-dried tomatoes, bell pepper, red onion, green onions, feta cheese, mint, Parmesan cheese, olives, and basil to the orzo mixture. Toss the salad with the vinaigrette. Season the salad to taste with more salt and pepper. Sprinkle the pine nuts over the salad. Garnish with teardrop tomatoes and Italian parsley leaves, and serve.

COOK'S NOTES: The vinaigrette, cooked asparagus and cooked orzo can be prepared 2 days ahead. Cover each separately and refrigerate. Once the salad has been tossed with the vinaigrette, it will keep for 1 day in the refrigerator.

Serves 6 to 8

BULGUR SALAD WITH FRESH MINT AND HEARTS OF ROMAINE

THIS HEALTHY AND FILLING SALAD IS COMMON IN VILLAGES OF THE MIDDLE EAST AND NORTH AFRICA. IT'S UNIQUELY BALANCED IN FLAVOR. SO MUCH SO, I FIND IT ADDICTIVE. ROLL THE SALAD IN LETTUCE LEAVES FOR A SNACK TIME TREAT! YOU'LL LOVE IT.

3/4 cup olive oil
2 large onions, finely chopped
1 (8-ounce) can tomato sauce
1 (6-ounce) can tomato paste
1 cup hot water
2 cups fine bulgur (#1 grade) (see page 12)
3 tablespoons fresh lemon juice
2 1/2 teaspoons salt, plus more to taste
1 1/2 teaspoons ground black pepper, plus more to taste
2 large tomatoes, seeded and finely chopped
1 red bell pepper, seeded and finely chopped
1 green bell pepper, seeded and finely chopped
6 green onions, chopped
1 cup finely chopped fresh mint
1 cup chopped fresh Italian parsley
5 hearts of romaine lettuce, cored, leaves separated

Heat the oil in a heavy large skillet over medium-high heat. Add the onions and sauté until they are soft but not brown, about 8 minutes. Stir in the tomato sauce and tomato paste. Remove the skillet from the heat. Stir in 1 cup of hot water, then the bulgur. Immediately cover the skillet tightly and let the mixture stand undisturbed until the bulgur is soft and the liquid is absorbed, about 10 minutes (do not remove the cover for at least 10 minutes). Transfer the bulgur mixture to a large bowl and cool to room temperature.

Stir the lemon juice, 2 1/2 teaspoons of salt, and 1 1/2 teaspoons of black pepper into the bulgur mixture. Add the chopped tomatoes, red and green bell peppers, green onions, parsley and mint, toss to combine. Season the salad to taste with more salt and pepper.

Spoon the bulgur salad into a large wide serving bowl, and surround it with the romaine lettuce leaves. Or, spoon some bulgur salad atop the romaine lettuce leaves and arrange them on a platter.

COOK'S NOTES: Another way I like to serve this is by spooning the bulgur salad in the centers of the hearts of romaine leaves and rolling them up like burritos.

You'll find that bulgur is numbered to indicate the coarseness of the grain (the higher the number, the courser the grain). Be sure to get the very fine grain for this recipe. The bulgur may be stored in the refrigerator for at least 3 months.

Serves 6 to 8

ROMAINE SALAD WITH HEARTS OF PALM AND ARTICHOKES

HEARTS OF PALM IS A VEGETABLE THAT COMES FROM PALMETTOS, SMALL PALM TREES THAT GROW IN FLORIDA AND ALSO IN PARTS OF SOUTH AMERICA. THE VEGETABLE HAS MANY LAYERS (SIMILAR TO LEEKS), A PALE IVORY COLOR, A MILD NUTTY FLAVOR, AND A SILKY TEXTURE. THEY ARE USED MOSTLY IN SALADS, SUCH AS THIS ONE. THEIR SLIGHTLY TART FLAVOR COMPLIMENTS THE SUN-DRIED TOMATO VINAIGRETTE, AND THEIR PLEASANT TEXTURE ADDS DIMENSION TO ANY LEAFY MIXED GREEN SALAD.

Sun-dried Tomato Vinaigrette

1/2 cup olive oil
1/4 cup red wine vinegar
1/4 cup sun-dried tomatoes packed in oil, drained and chopped
1 teaspoon minced fresh garlic
1 teaspoon ground black pepper
1 teaspoon salt

Salad

1 (14-ounce) can artichoke hearts, drained, rinsed and patted dry
1 (14-ounce) can hearts of palm, drained, rinsed and patted dry
7 cups coarsely chopped romaine lettuce (from 1 head)
1 small red onion, very thinly sliced (about 1 cup)
1/2 cup coarsely chopped fresh Italian parsley
1 (12-ounce) basket cherry or grape tomatoes, halved
1 ounce Parmesan cheese, shaved

To make the sun-dried tomato vinaigrette: Combine the oil, vinegar, sun-dried tomatoes, garlic, black pepper and salt in a large jar. Seal the jar and shake until the dressing is well blended.

To make the salad: Quarter the artichoke hearts, and cut the hearts of palm diagonally into 1/2-inch-thick slices. Combine the artichoke hearts and hearts of palm in a large bowl. Add the lettuce, onion, and parsley. Cover and refrigerate until the salad is cold.

Toss the salad with the tomatoes and enough vinaigrette to coat. Season the salad to taste with more salt and pepper. Sprinkle the Parmesan cheese shavings over and serve immediately.

COOK'S NOTES: If you cannot find canned artichoke hearts, substitute marinated artichokes that come in a jar. It is not absolutely necessary to have hearts of palm in this salad, but they do add a wonderful taste and texture to the salad.

Be sure the ingredients are chilled before tossing the salad with the vinaigrette. Try adding Kalamata olives, feta cheese, or sliced radishes. Serve the salad with crusty bread and Chianti wine.

The dressing is basic but very tasty, and perks up any simple steamed vegetables.

Serves 6 to 8

GRILLED ZA-ATAR-COATED CHICKEN WITH MIXED BABY GREENS

ZA-ATAR, A DARK-GREEN MIXTURE OF THYME, TOASTED SESAME SEEDS, AND GROUND SUMAC, IS TRADITIONALLY MIXED WITH OLIVE OIL AND SERVED AS A DIP OR SPREAD OVER BREAD SLICES. ZA ATAR (ALSO SPELLED ZA'ATAR) IS AVAILABLE AT LOCAL ETHNIC MARKETS BUT CAN BE MADE FROM SCRATCH BY COMBINING EQUAL PARTS OF GROUND, DRIED THYME AND TOASTED SESAME SEEDS, WITH A LITTLE BIT OF SUMAC (ABOUT ONE-FOURTH OF THE AMOUNT OF THE OTHER INGREDIENTS), AND SALT TO TASTE. THE WONDERFULLY TART FLAVOR OF SUMAC BALANCES AND COMPLEMENTS THE OTHER SEASONINGS, RESULTING IN VERY UNIQUE AND DELICIOUS GRILLED CHICKEN.

6 boneless skinless chicken breasts
3 teaspoons salt
2 teaspoons ground black pepper
3/4 cup za-atar (page 14)
4 tablespoons plus 1 teaspoon olive oil
2 ears of corn, kernels cut from cob
2 cups canned fava beans, rinsed,
  drained and patted dry
2 tomatoes, seeded and cut into 1/2-inch pieces
1 red bell pepper, seeded and cut into 1/2-inch pieces
1 green bell pepper, seeded and cut into 1/2-inch pieces
2 tablespoons minced fresh shallots
3 tablespoons fresh lemon juice
6 cups mixed baby greens

Sprinkle the chicken with 1 1/2 teaspoons of salt and 1 teaspoon of black pepper. Stir the za-atar and 3 tablespoons of oil in a small bowl to blend. Rub the herb mixture all over the chicken. Cover and refrigerate at least 1 hour or up to1 day.

Prepare the barbecue for medium-high heat. Grill the chicken until just cooked through, about 4 minutes per side. Set the chicken aside and cool. Cut the chicken into 1/4-inch-thick strips.

Toss the corn kernels, fava beans, tomatoes, red and green bell peppers, and shallots in a large bowl. Whisk the lemon juice, 1 tablespoon of oil, 1 1/2 teaspoons of salt, and 1 teaspoon of black pepper in a small bowl to blend. Drizzle the dressing over the vegetable mixture and toss to coat. Toss the mixed greens with the remaining 1 teaspoon of oil in another large bowl.

Place a bed of the mixed greens on each plate. Mound the vegetable mixture on top of the greens. Top with the sliced chicken pieces and serve.

COOK'S NOTES: During the spring, when fresh fava beans are available, use them in place of the canned beans. They do require a bit more work, but their fresh flavor and pale green color add to the beauty of this salad. To prepare fresh fava beans, remove them from their large pods, and cook the beans in boiling water for 1 minute. Then, peel away the outer shell from the bean. One pound of whole fava beans will yield about 1/2 cup of peeled fresh beans.

When grilling chicken, cook the meat fairly close to the heat source. This method of cooking seals the juices in so that the meat becomes more tender and succulent. A chicken breast is cooked perfectly when the center is heated to 160°F (you can use a meat thermometer); if you exceed that temperature, the chicken is considered over-cooked and will most likely yield a stringy and tough texture.

Serves 6

CANNELLINI AND GARBANZO BEAN SALAD WITH OVEN-ROASTED TOMATOES

THE WONDERFUL THING ABOUT THIS SALAD IS THAT IT GOES BEAUTIFULLY WITH SEAFOOD, SUCH AS GRILLED OR SAUTÉED SHRIMP, TUNA OR SALMON. I LOVE IT AS A VEGETARIAN ENTRÉE, ESPECIALLY WHEN SERVED ON A BED OF TENDER MIXED BABY GREENS. THIS SALAD IS BEST SERVED AT ROOM TEMPERATURE; IT ALSO MAKES A GREAT SALAD FOR PICNICS, BARBECUES AND OTHER OUTDOOR PARTIES.

3 tablespoons olive oil
3 tablespoons thinly sliced fresh basil
1 3/4 teaspoons salt, plus more to taste
3/4 teaspoon ground black pepper, plus more to taste
3 plum tomatoes, halved lengthwise
1 1/4 pounds white mushrooms or
  stemmed shiitake mushrooms, sliced
1 large Japanese eggplant, cut into 1/2-inch pieces
2 cups canned cannellini beans,
  rinsed, drained and patted dry
1 cup canned garbanzo beans, rinsed,
  drained and patted dry
1 small zucchini, halved lengthwise and
  thinly sliced crosswise
1/2 cup thinly sliced green bell pepper
1/2 cup thinly sliced red bell pepper
1/2 cup thinly sliced red onion
2 green onions, thinly sliced diagonally
3 tablespoons chopped fresh cilantro
3 tablespoons chopped fresh Italian parsley
3 tablespoons chopped fresh mint
1/4 cup fresh lemon juice
  Pinch of dried crushed red pepper

Preheat the oven to 475°F. Line a baking sheet with foil. Whisk 1 tablespoon of oil, 1 tablespoon of basil, 1/4 teaspoon of salt, and 1/4 teaspoon of black pepper in a medium bowl. Add the tomatoes and toss to coat. Place the tomatoes, cut side up, on the prepared baking sheet. Spoon any remaining oil mixture over the tomatoes. Bake just until the skins loosen from the tomatoes (do not overcook), about 5 minutes. Set aside until the tomatoes are cool enough to handle. Peel the tomatoes, then cut each tomato diagonally into 3 slices. Transfer the tomatoes to a large bowl. Cool completely.

Meanwhile, heat 2 tablespoons of oil in a heavy large skillet over medium–high heat. Add mushrooms and sauté until they are golden brown, about 10 minutes. Add the eggplant and sauté until soft, about 5 minutes more. Set aside to cool completely.

Toss the mushroom mixture, cannellini beans, garbanzo beans, zucchini, green and red bell peppers, red onion, green onions, cilantro, parsley, mint, and the remaining 2 tablespoons of basil with the tomatoes in the large bowl. Add the lemon juice, crushed red pepper, and remaining 1 1/2 teaspoons of salt and 1/2 teaspoon of black pepper. Toss again to combine. Season the salad to taste with more salt and pepper, if desired. Serve the salad at room temperature.

COOK'S NOTES: This salad can be prepared 1 day ahead. Cover and refrigerate it, then bring it to room temperature before serving.

Any variety of mushrooms will work in this crowd pleaser. Try it with stemmed shiitake, crimini or portobello mushrooms.

Serves 8 to 10

BAGHDAD, IRAQ 1954

In the city's main section, our elementary
school stretches along a cement wall that separates the
schoolyard grounds from an old cemetery—above-
ground tombs situated in even rows that we passed
each day when our teachers released us for daily prayers.
A sudden, roaring river of 10-year-olds, we flooded
the dusty yard, but veered sharply from the path to the
church in back of the school. Far to the right stood
the lunchroom—a plain, narrow structure with a low
ceiling and black bars on the screen-less windows.

Behind the shack's back counter Baydzar Mora
stands confidently, expecting us. Huge in her dark
dress and scarf pulled tightly around her head like a
pirate, she is no ordinary cook; we think of her as
the Grand Dame, a culinary whiz. Aunt Sunshine, as
her name translates from Armenian, firmly commands
us—hundreds of children who have packed into the
building—to maintain order as we anxiously await
our turn to buy delicious Piaz, a sandwich of fresh
potato salad in homemade bread.

The rich aroma of mango chutney permeates the
air that, with the Iraqi desert's temperature, grows
hotter and hotter, rising well into the hundreds.
But our mouths moisten in anticipation of the spicy
curry we know will cool us. The chutney or "amba" is
the magic that adds zest to the Piaz—salty, slightly sour
potatoes of firm texture mixed with golden olive oil,
freshly chopped mint and parsley, all stuffed into the
belly of just-baked bread that crackles with each bite.

ZOV'S FAVORITE POTATO SALAD

WHEN I WANT TO PREPARE A POTATO SALAD, I THINK OF THE PIAZ–A MEDITERRANEAN POTATO SALAD. A HARMONY OF FRESH AND DRIED MINT REALLY DISTINGUISHES IT FROM ANY OTHER. CONSISTENTLY DELICIOUS AND UTTERLY UNIQUE, THIS IS GREAT FOR PICNICS SINCE IT IS SERVED AT ROOM TEMPERATURE. SERVE IT AS A SIDE DISH TO GRILLED SIRLOIN BURGERS AND ROSEMARY GARLIC CHICKEN (PAGE 185), OR IN A FRENCH ROLL TOPPED WITH AMBA (PICKLED MANGO CHUTNEY) AS I DID AS A CHILD.

2 pounds small red-skinned potatoes,
   cut into 3/4-inch pieces
1/3 cup fresh lemon juice
1/3 cup olive oil (see Cook's Notes)
2 1/2 teaspoons salt, plus more to taste
1 teaspoon ground black pepper, plus more to taste
1 teaspoon crushed dried mint
1/3 cup finely chopped green onions
1/3 cup finely chopped red onion
3 tablespoons finely chopped fresh mint
   Fresh mint sprigs, for garnish

Fill a large pot with enough water to come 2 inches up the sides of the pot. Place a steamer basket in the pot. Cover the pot and bring the water to a boil. Place the potatoes in the basket and steam until they are just tender, stirring after the first 4 minutes. about 8 minutes total. Remove the potatoes from the pot.

Meanwhile, whisk the lemon juice, oil, 2 1/2 teaspoons of salt, 1 teaspoon of black pepper, and dried mint in a large bowl to blend. Add the drained hot potatoes and toss to coat. Add green onions, red onions and chopped fresh mint. Toss gently to combine. Set the salad aside until it is room temperature, tossing occasionally. Season the salad to taste with salt and pepper. Garnish the salad with fresh mint sprigs and serve.

Serves 4 to 6

COOK'S NOTES: This salad is very simple to put together, but there are keys within the steps to making it great. First of all, the potatoes must be warm when tossed with the other ingredients, and there must be an equal balance of salt and lemon juice. Be sure to use a good-quality extra-virgin olive oil, to impart a significant flavor. Don't worry if the salad looks too moist, the warm potatoes will absorb the lemon juice and oil. Season the salad again just before serving, since the potatoes absorb the salt and seasonings as they cool.

You can find amba at any Indian market sold as pickled mango chutney.

GREEK SALAD

THIS RECIPE IS PROBABLY MORE
ROBUST THAN ORDINARY GREEK SALADS.
IT IS IMPORTANT TO USE THE FRESHEST
INGREDIENTS. TOSS THE SALAD JUST BEFORE
SERVING, AND USE A HIGH-QUALITY OLIVE
OIL IN ORDER TO BRING OUT THE SALAD'S
DRAMATIC POTENTIAL. THE DRIED MINT IS
PARTICULARLY SIGNIFICANT, AS IT GIVES THE
SALAD A LAYER OF REFRESHING COOLNESS.

2 hothouse cucumbers (about 1 1/2 pounds total),
   seeded and cut into 1/2-inch chunks (see Cook's Notes)
6 plum tomatoes, 4 cut into 6 wedges each,
2 coarsely chopped
4 green onions, thinly sliced diagonally
1 small red onion, thinly sliced
4 ounces feta cheese, cut into 1/4-inch cubes
1/2 cup Kalamata olives (pitted optional)
1/3 cup chopped fresh Italian parsley
1/4 cup thinly sliced fresh mint
1/3 cup fresh lemon juice
1/3 cup olive oil
1 1/2 teaspoons salt
1 teaspoon crushed dried mint
1 teaspoon ground black pepper
1 teaspoon seasoned salt

Toss the cucumbers, tomatoes, green onions, red
onion, feta cheese, olives, parsley, and fresh mint in
a large bowl. Whisk the lemon juice, oil, black pepper,
dried mint, seasoned salt, and salt in a small bowl to
blend. Toss the salad with the dressing to coat.
Serve immediately.

Serving Suggestions: Top the salad with grilled chicken
breast or leftover rotisserie chicken for a satisfying
entrée. If doubled, this salad makes a great buffet item
for serving to large groups. For a unique and pretty
presentation, hollow out the centers of heads of butter
lettuce, and spoon the salad into the centers.

COOK'S NOTES: Different cucumbers will yield very
different textures to the salad. Be sure to select ones
that are crisp and firm. Japanese cucumbers are a good
choice for this salad because they are firm and very
crisp. You can use the regular cucumbers as well, but
be sure to peel and seed them first.

Serves 6 to 8

ASPARAGUS AND MUSHROOM SALAD WITH POMEGRANATE VINAIGRETTE

SHIITAKE MUSHROOMS ARE NOT ONLY DELICIOUS, THEY'RE QUITE HEARTY. UNLIKE OTHER MUSHROOMS, THEY KEEP THEIR MEATY TEXTURE WHEN COOKED, AND THEIR FLAVOR LENDS A PARTICULAR VIVIDNESS TO THE ASPARAGUS AND GRILLED PEPPERS. CREMINI MUSHROOMS WILL WORK, TOO, THOUGH I PREFER THE SHIITAKE.

Pomegranate Vinaigrette

1 tablespoon pomegranate molasses (page 13)
1 tablespoon balsamic vinegar
1/2 teaspoon ground black pepper, plus more to taste
1/2 teaspoon salt, plus more to taste
3 tablespoons olive oil

Salad

1 1/2 pounds asparagus, trimmed
1 red bell pepper
1 yellow bell pepper
2 tablespoons butter
2 tablespoons olive oil
8 ounces shiitake mushrooms, stemmed and sliced
2 tablespoons minced garlic
1 small red onion, thinly sliced
2 tomatoes, cut into 1/2-inch pieces (rough diced)
  Salt and ground black pepper, to taste
1/4 cup thinly sliced fresh basil

To make the pomegranate vinaigrette: Whisk the pomegranate molasses, vinegar, and 1/2 teaspoon each of black pepper and salt and in a medium bowl to blend. Gradually whisk in the oil. Season the dressing to taste with more salt and black pepper.

To make the salad: Cut the asparagus crosswise in half, then cut each piece lengthwise in half. Bring a large saucepan of water to a boil. Add the asparagus and cook just until it turns bright green, about 30 seconds. Immediately transfer the asparagus to a large bowl of ice water. Let stand until cold. Drain the asparagus and pat completely dry.

Roast the red and yellow bell peppers over a gas flame until lightly charred all over, about 10 minutes. Enclose the peppers in a plastic bag until cool enough to handle. Peel, seed and slice the peppers into 1/4-inch-wide strips. Pat the peppers dry to remove any excess liquid.

Melt the butter and oil in a heavy large skillet over medium-high heat. Add the mushrooms and sauté for 2 minutes. Reduce the heat to medium. Add the garlic and sauté until the liquid from the mushrooms evaporates and the mushrooms and garlic are golden brown, about 5 minutes. Transfer the mushrooms to a large bowl and cool to room temperature. Add the cooked asparagus, roasted peppers, onion, and tomatoes to the mushrooms. Cover and refrigerate until the salad is cold.

Toss the salad with enough vinaigrette to coat, and season to taste with salt and pepper. Mound the salad on a platter. Sprinkle with the basil and serve.

COOK'S NOTES: Immersing asparagus in ice water stops it from cooking and prevents it from discoloration. To keep the colors bright, toss the salad with the vinaigrette just before serving.

Serves 6

COUSCOUS SALAD WITH GRILLED CHICKEN AND SPICY MUSTARD VINAIGRETTE

THIS HEARTY SALAD MAKES A GREAT PARTY DISH. FOR A LUNCHEON FARE, I LIKE TO ARRANGE MIXED BABY GREENS OVER THE BOTTOM OF INDIVIDUAL SALAD PLATES, THEN MOUND THIS FABULOUS COUSCOUS ATOP THE GREENS, AND FAN THE CHICKEN SLICES OVER THE COUSCOUS. A CRISP CHENIN BLANC WINE PAIRS PARTICULARLY WELL WITH THIS SALAD. WITHOUT THE CHICKEN, IT MAKES AN EXCELLENT VEGETARIAN ENTRÉE. OTHER MEATS WORK WELL WITH THE COUSCOUS, TOO. GET CREATIVE!

Spicy Mustard Vinaigrette

6 garlic cloves
1/2 cup rice vinegar
2 tablespoons Dijon mustard
1 tablespoon salt
1 1/2 teaspoons seasoned salt
1/2 teaspoon dried crushed red pepper
1/2 teaspoon ground black pepper
1/2 cup olive oil

Chicken and Couscous Salad

1 tablespoon minced garlic
1 tablespoon chopped fresh rosemary leaves
1 1/2 teaspoons salt, plus more to taste
1 teaspoon ground black pepper, plus more to taste
7 tablespoons olive oil
6 boneless skinless chicken breasts
1 pound Israeli couscous (see Cook's Notes)
2 large onions, halved lengthwise and sliced crosswise
1 1/2 pounds asparagus, trimmed,
   cut diagonally into 3/4-inch lengths and blanched
4 large carrots, peeled
   cut into 1/3-inch pieces and blanched
4 medium zucchini, halved lengthwise,
   thinly sliced diagonally and blanched
2 red bell peppers, roasted, seeded and
   cut into thin strips
2 yellow bell peppers, roasted, seeded and
   cut into thin strips
1 (15-ounce) can garbanzo beans, drained,
   rinsed and patted dry
1 cup golden raisins or currants
3/4 cup pitted Kalamata olives

To make the spicy mustard vinaigrette: Mince the garlic in a food processor. Blend in the vinegar, mustard, salt, seasoned salt, crushed red pepper, and black pepper. With the machine running, gradually blend in the oil. Cover and refrigerate the vinaigrette.

To grill the chicken: Prepare the barbecue for medium-high heat. Whisk the garlic, rosemary, 1 1/2 teaspoons salt, 1 teaspoon black pepper, and 2 tablespoons of oil in a small bowl to blend. Rub the oil mixture over the chicken breasts. Grill the chicken until they are just cooked through, about 4 minutes per side. Transfer the chicken to a platter and refrigerate until it is cold. Cut the chicken breasts crosswise into thin slices. Cover and refrigerate the chicken.

To make the couscous salad: Bring a large pot of water to a boil over high heat. Add the couscous. Return the water to a boil and cook until the couscous is al dente, stirring occasionally, about 5 minutes. Do not over-cook the couscous, since it will soften further as it cools. Drain the couscous well, then transfer it to a large bowl, and toss it with 2 tablespoons of oil to coat. Cool the couscous to room temperature.

Meanwhile, heat the remaining 3 tablespoons of oil in a heavy large skillet over high heat. Add the onions and sauté until they are brown and caramelized, about 15 minutes. Cool completely.

Add the onions, asparagus, carrots, zucchini, red and yellow bell peppers, garbanzo beans, and raisins to the couscous. (The vinaigrette, chicken and couscous salad can be made up to this point at least 1 day ahead. Cover each separately and keep them refrigerated. Re-whisk the vinaigrette before using.)

Just before serving, toss the salad with enough vinaigrette to moisten. Season to taste with more salt and pepper. Transfer the salad to a large serving bowl or platter. Arrange the sliced chicken atop the salad. Garnish with the olives and serve.

COOK'S NOTES: Israeli couscous is larger than regular couscous, with a diameter about the size of black peppercorns. It is sometimes labeled as pearl couscous. It's available at Middle Eastern markets, and Natural foods stores, and some specialty foods stores. If you can't find it, use regular couscous or orzo (rice-shaped pasta) instead, and follow the cooking directions on the package.

Blanching is a simple technique that helps tenderize vegetables and brighten their colors. To blanch the asparagus, carrots, and zucchini, simply submerge them in a large saucepan of boiling water just until their colors brighten, about 30 seconds for the asparagus and zucchini, and about 2 minutes for the carrots. Once the vegetables are cooked, drain them and immediately submerge them in a large bowl of ice water. This will stop them from cooking and preserve their vivid colors. Be sure to dry the vegetables well so that the water does not dilute the salad.

Serves 12 to 14.

LENTIL SALAD WITH ARUGULA AND LEMON VINAIGRETTE

LENTILS ARE A COMPLETE PROTEIN, EASY TO DIGEST, AND VERY FILLING. COMBINED WITH FETA CHEESE, FRESH HERBS, AND VEGETABLES THEY BECOME A DELIGHTFUL SUMMER SALAD THAT EVERY "BODY" WILL LOVE. SERVE THE SALAD ON ITS OWN FOR A LIGHT LUNCH, OR WITH POACHED SALMON OR ANY TYPE OF GRILLED MEATS FOR A HEARTIER MEAL. THE DELICIOUS LEMONY VINAIGRETTE CAN BE USED ON OTHER SALADS, FROM LEAFY GREENS TO PASTA SALADS. REFRIGERATE ANY LEFTOVER VINAIGRETTE IN A JAR WITH A TIGHT-FITTING LID UP TO ONE WEEK.

Lemon Vinaigrette

1/4 cup fresh lemon juice
3 tablespoons white wine vinegar
1 garlic clove, minced
1 tablespoon minced shallot
1 teaspoon ground black pepper
1 teaspoon salt
1/4 cup olive oil

Salad

1/2 teaspoon salt
1 1/2 cups dried green lentils
3 tablespoons olive oil
3 celery stalks, thinly sliced diagonally
2 yellow crookneck squash, thinly sliced diagonally
8 green onions, thinly sliced diagonally
1 small red onion, thinly sliced
1 red bell pepper, seeded and cut into matchstick-size strips
1 carrot, peeled and thinly sliced diagonally
1/2 cup chopped fresh cilantro
1/2 cup chopped fresh Italian parsley
2 cups red and yellow teardrop tomatoes, halved
1 1/2 cups (about 1 1/2 ounces) baby arugula or spinach, coarsely chopped
1 cup crumbled feta cheese

To make the lemon vinaigrette: Whisk the lemon juice, vinegar, garlic, shallot, black pepper, and salt in a large bowl to blend. Gradually whisk in the oil. Set the vinaigrette aside.

To make the salad: Bring 3 cups of water and the salt to a boil in a large saucepan. Add the lentils. Reduce the heat to medium-low. Cover and simmer gently until the lentils are just tender, about 15 minutes. Drain well. Toss the lentils with the oil in a large bowl to coat. Cool completely.

Toss the lentils with the celery, squash, green onions, red onion, bell pepper, carrot, cilantro, and parsley. Add the tomatoes, arugula, and feta cheese. "At this point, the salad will keep for 1 to 2 days, covered and refrigerated." Whisk the vinaigrette again to blend, then toss the salad with enough vinaigrette to coat. Season the salad to taste with more salt and pepper, and serve.

COOK'S NOTES: This is a wonderful salad for entertaining. Once the salad is completely assembled, it will keep for 1 day, covered in the refrigerator.

A few lentils go a long way. As they cook, they expand to three times their original volume! Watch the lentils as they cook to make sure they do not overcook, as they tend to become very mushy quickly. If cooked just right, though, they are so delicious!

For a variation, substitute the teardrop tomatoes with sun-dried tomatoes or add marinated artichoke hearts.

Serves 6 to 8

HEIRLOOM TOMATO SALAD WITH GRILLED EGGPLANT AND PEPPERS

GET CREATIVE WITH YOUR FAVORITE VEGETABLES WHEN ASSEMBLING THIS SALAD. I SUGGEST EXPERIMENTING WITH GRILLED ZUCCHINI OR MUSHROOMS. WHEN HEIRLOOM TOMATOES ARE NOT IN SEASON, USE YELLOW AND RED TEARDROP TOMATOES. THEY'LL GIVE THIS SALAD A SWEET TASTE AND VERY BALANCED COMPOSITION. FOR AN ATTRACTIVE PRESENTATION, SLICE ADDITIONAL HEIRLOOM TOMATOES AND ARRANGE THEM IN A CONCENTRIC CIRCLE ON SERVING PLATES, THEN SPOON THE SALAD ATOP THE SLICED TOMATOES. SERVE THIS SALAD AS A FIRST COURSE OR PAIR IT WITH CHILLED STEAMED CRAB CLAWS OR GRILLED CHICKEN, SHRIMP, OR HALIBUT FOR A DELICIOUS ENTRÉE.

5 tablespoons olive oil
2 eggplants (2 pounds total),
  cut crosswise into 3/4-inch-thick slices
1 red bell pepper, halved lengthwise and seeded
1 green bell pepper, halved lengthwise and seeded
1 teaspoon ground black pepper, plus more to taste
1 teaspoon salt, plus more to taste
1/4 cup balsamic vinegar
2 garlic cloves, minced
4 heirloom tomatoes (about 1 1/2 pounds total),
  cut into 3/4-inch cubes
3/4 cup chopped green onions
1/2 cup finely chopped red onion
1/2 cup coarsely chopped fresh mint
1/3 cup coarsely chopped fresh basil
1/4 cup coarsely chopped fresh Italian parsley
4 ounces feta cheese, very coarsely crumbled

Prepare the barbecue for medium-high heat. Brush 3 tablespoons of oil over both sides of the eggplant slices and the red and green bell peppers. Sprinkle the eggplants and bell peppers with 1 teaspoon each of black pepper and salt. Grill until they are tender and grill marks appear, about 10 minutes. Transfer the vegetables to a large baking sheet to cool completely. Cut the vegetables into 1/2-inch pieces.

Whisk the remaining 2 tablespoons of oil, vinegar, and garlic in a large bowl to blend. Add the grilled vegetables, tomatoes, green onions, red onion, mint, basil, and parsley, and toss to combine. Add the feta cheese and toss gently to combine. Season the salad to taste with salt and pepper, and serve at room temperature

COOK'S NOTES: This salad is best served soon after it is tossed together. However, the grilled eggplant and peppers can be prepared 1 day ahead. Keep them covered and refrigerated, then bring them to room temperature before tossing with the remaining ingredients. Never refrigerate the tomatoes, as this seriously diminishes their prized freshness and flavor.

I like to use French feta cheese because it has a milder flavor and truly gives a nice balance to the grilled vegetables. I've also found that soft, fresh goat cheese makes an excellent substitute for the feta.

Serves 6 to 8

SPINACH SALAD WITH SMOKED TURKEY, AND GREEN APPLE VINAIGRETTE

CRISP TART APPLES AND TOASTED WALNUTS MAKE A FABULOUS PAIR IN THIS FLAVORFUL, MULTI-TEXTURED SALAD. TOSS THE SALAD JUST BEFORE SERVING. YOU CAN SUBSTITUTE MIXED BABY GREENS INSTEAD OF SPINACH, IF YOU'D LIKE. SERVE IT FOR A LUNCHEON WITH A CHILLED CRISP SAUVIGNON BLANC OR CHARDONNAY.

Green Apple Vinaigrette
1/2 Granny Smith apple, cored and coarsely chopped
1/3 cup sherry vinegar
1/4 cup apple juice
3 tablespoons honey
3 tablespoons minced shallots
1 tablespoon whole grain Dijon mustard
2 teaspoons salt
1 teaspoon freshly ground black pepper
2/3 cup vegetable oil or canola

Salad
1 pound smoked turkey, cut into matchstick-size strips
8 ounces smoked Gouda cheese,
   cut into matchstick-size strips
1 large Granny Smith apple, cored and
   cut into matchstick-size strips
2 celery stalks, thinly sliced diagonally
1/2 small red onion, very thinly sliced
10 ounces fresh baby spinach
   (about 8 lightly packed cups)
   salt and ground black pepper, to taste
2 plum tomatoes, seeded and finely diced
1 1/3 cups walnuts, toasted and
   coarsely chopped (page 18)
1 Red-Delicious apple, cored and thinly sliced

To make the green apple vinaigrette: Blend all the ingredients, except the oil, in a food processor. With the machine running, gradually blend in the oil. In a thin stream.

To make the salad: Toss the turkey, cheese, green apple, celery, and onion in a large bowl with enough vinaigrette to coat lightly. Toss the spinach in another large bowl with enough vinaigrette to coat lightly. Season the spinach to taste with salt and pepper.

Arrange a bed of spinach atop of each plate. Mound the turkey salad atop the spinach. Sprinkle the tomatoes then the walnuts over the salads. Arrange the red apple slices around the salads and serve.

COOK'S NOTES: Choose apples that are firm and crisp. To keep the apples from turning brown after they are sliced, toss them with 1 teaspoon of orange juice or lemon juice.

Serves 8 to 10

WHEAT BERRY SALAD WITH GARBANZO BEANS

IF YOU'RE IN THE MOOD FOR A HEALTHY AND HEARTY VEGETARIAN SALAD , THIS IS THE ONE FOR YOU. IT ALSO WORKS AS A PERFECT SIDE DISH TO GRILLED SEAFOOD, BEEF, OR CHICKEN. THE LIST BELOW LOOKS LONG, BUT ALL OF THE ITEMS ARE READILY AVAILABLE IN MOST KITCHENS.

1 1/2 cups hot water
1 cup coarse bulgur (#4 grade) (page 12)
3 tablespoons plus 1/2 cup olive oil
8 ounces white mushrooms, sliced
2 tablespoons minced garlic
1 (15 1/2-ounce) can garbanzo beans, rinsed,
  drained and patted dry
1 red bell pepper, thinly sliced
1 yellow bell pepper, thinly sliced
1 cup thinly sliced celery
1 cup thinly sliced green onions
3/4 cup chopped fresh mint
2 small carrots, peeled and very thinly sliced
1/2 red onion, thinly sliced
2 tablespoons chopped fresh thyme
1/2 cup fresh lemon juice
2 teaspoons ground black pepper, plus more to taste
2 teaspoons salt, plus more to taste

Combine the hot water and bulgur in a heavy medium saucepan. Bring the water to a boil over high heat. Reduce the heat to medium-low. Cover and simmer gently until the water is absorbed and the bulgur is almost tender, about 15 minutes. Set aside to cool.

Meanwhile, heat 3 tablespoons of oil in a heavy large skillet over medium-high heat. Add the mushrooms and sauté for 2 minutes. Reduce the heat to medium. Add the garlic and sauté until the liquid from the mushrooms evaporates and the mushrooms and garlic are golden brown, about 5 minutes. Transfer the mushrooms to a large bowl and cool.

Add the cooked bulgur, garbanzo beans, red and yellow bell peppers, celery, green onion, mint, carrots, red onion, and thyme to the mushrooms in the large bowl. Whisk the remaining 1/2 cup of oil, lemon juice, and 2 teaspoons of each black pepper and salt in a medium bowl to blend. Pour the dressing over the bulgur mixture and toss to coat. Season the salad to taste with more salt and black pepper. Serve the salad at room temperature.

COOK'S NOTES: This salad keeps for 1 day, covered and refrigerated.

Serves 6 to 8

CABBAGE SALAD WITH MINT AND CILANTRO

THIS ASIAN-INSPIRED SALAD IS VERY REFRESHING, AND MAKES A WONDERFUL CHANGE FROM TRADITIONAL COLESLAW. TRY IT AS A UNIQUE CONDIMENT ON THE SALMON BURGER (PAGE 209) OR SERVE IT WITH THE SESAME CRUSTED SALMON (PAGE 212) AND ANY GRILLED POULTRY, SEAFOOD, OR MEAT.

1/2 head of green cabbage, thinly sliced (about 5 cups)
1 cucumber, peeled, seeded and
  cut into matchstick-size strips
1 small red bell pepper, seeded and thinly sliced
1 small red onion, very thinly sliced (about 1 cup)
3 green onions, thinly sliced diagonally
1/2 cup lightly packed fresh cilantro leaves,
  coarsely chopped
1/2 cup lightly packed fresh mint leaves, thinly sliced
1/4 cup fresh lime juice
2 tablespoons fresh lemon juice
2 tablespoons rice vinegar
2 tablespoons sugar
3/4 teaspoon salt
  Mint sprigs, for garnish
  Cilantro sprigs, for garnish

Combine the cabbage, cucumber, bell pepper, red onion, green onions, cilantro, and mint in a large bowl.

Whisk the lime juice, lemon juice, vinegar, sugar, and salt in a medium bowl until the sugar and salt dissolve. Pour the lime juice mixture over the cabbage mixture and toss to coat. Garnish the coleslaw with fresh mint and cilantro sprigs and serve.

COOK'S NOTE: The cabbage mixture and lime juice mixture can be made 1 day ahead. Cover separately and refrigerate

Serves 4 to 6

CAPER VINAIGRETTE

ONE OF THE GREAT PLEASURES AT ZOV'S BISTRO IS THIS CAPER VINAIGRETTE, IT EMULSIFIES INTO THIS RICH, THICK DRESSING, FILLED WITH THE FLAVOR OF FRESH LEMONS AND THE CAPERS. A DELICIOUS DRESSING FOR COBB SALAD AND ANY GREEN LEAF LETTUCE.

Makes 1 2/3 cups

1/3 cup red wine vinegar
1/4 cup finely chopped shallots
3 tablespoons capers plus 2 tablespoons juice
3 tablespoons finely chopped fresh Italian parsley
2 tablespoons Dijon mustard
1 large egg yolk
1 teaspoon ground black pepper
1 teaspoon salt
1/2 cup canola oil

Blend the vinegar, shallots, capers and juice, parsley, mustard, egg yolk, black pepper, and salt in a blender until almost smooth. Slowly add the oil in a drizzle while the machine is running.

COOK'S NOTES: The vinaigrette will keep up to 3 days. Store it in a glass jar with a tight-fitting lid and keep it refrigerated.

BALSAMIC POMEGRANATE VINAIGRETTE

SERVE ON MIXED BABY GREENS OR FRESH BABY SPINACH SALAD. IT IS TERRIFIC SERVED ON FRESH BABY BEETS.

Makes 1 1/2 cups

1/4 cup balsamic vinegar
1/4 cup rice vinegar
4 garlic cloves
2 tablespoons Dijon mustard
2 tablespoons finely chopped shallots
2 tablespoons pure maple syrup
1 tablespoon pomegranate molasses
1 1/2 teaspoons salt
1 teaspoon ground black pepper
1/2 cup canola oil

Blend balsamic vinegar, rice vinegar, garlic, mustard, shallots, maple syrup, molasses, salt, and pepper in a blender until smooth. With the machine running, gradually pour the oil in a thin stream.

COOK'S NOTES: The vinaigrette will keep up to 3 days. Store it in a glass jar with a tight-fitting lid and keep it refrigerated.

CAESAR
SALAD DRESSING

CAESAR IS ONE OF THE MOST REQUESTED
SALADS WE SERVE IN OUR RESTAURANT.
YOU CAN SUBSTITUTE CAYENNE PEPPER
INSTEAD OF BLACK PEPPER FOR
STRONGER HEAT

Makes 1 1/2 cups
10 garlic cloves
1/4 cup white wine vinegar
1 large egg yolk
3 tablespoons fresh lemon juice
2 tablespoons Dijon mustard
8 canned anchovy fillets, drained
1/2 cup vegetable oil
1 teaspoon ground black pepper
1 teaspoon salt
1 teaspoon Worcestershire sauce
1/2 teaspoon hot pepper sauce (such as Tabasco)

Blend the garlic, vinegar, egg yolk, lemon juice,
mustard, and anchovies in a blender until smooth.
With the machine running, gradually pour in the oil.
Blend in the black pepper, salt, Worcestershire
sauce, and hot pepper sauce.

COOK'S NOTES: The dressing will keep up to 3 days.
Store it in a glass jar with a tight-fitting lid and keep
it refrigerated. For variation or if you want a rich
and creamy Caesar salad, add 1/2 cup of crumbled
Roquefort cheese to the dressing.

SOUPS

These delicious soup recipes incorporate traditional spice combinations that give them special flair, like the much-sought-after Golden Lentil Soup for which my patrons drive many miles again and again. Your family and guests will love these soups!

TUSTIN, CALIFORNIA 1987

I recall one of those early days when my mother had come to help me deal with the pressures of opening my new restaurant. "Which soup shall we offer?" I asked her, having pondered the subject for weeks. She smiled, and with that knowing look all mothers possess, said, "Your favorite, of course." Of course! Yet, I resisted. My mother's Golden Lentil Soup had been my personal indulgence, my comfort since I was a young girl. It seemed too much a part of my home, too simple a dish. But my mother insisted. Today the Golden Lentil Soup remains our signature soup—sought after by many for its therapeutic powers.

The beauty of the soup is in the subtle, exotic spices that transport you around the world and, most importantly, back home again. The lentils, rosy orange when dry, turn deep gold when cooked—the color of the desert sands of the Middle East. The soup's red pepper undertones are reminiscent of the busy spice market of Istanbul. The cumin, one of my favorite spices, harmonizes with the red pepper. Each time I taste it, I am transported back to the souks of Fez, Morocco, walking down narrow, winding aisles walled by rows of barrels and jars full of coarsely ground spices of all colors: fire red, deep orange, amber, champagne, turmeric, anise, sumac and chili pepper. I am crowded by shoppers, equally colorful, who dominate the store's hot open space.

Onion imbues the lentil soup with the tender sweetness of familiarity, and I am no longer at Zov's Bistro. I am back home again in my mother's kitchen. She stands at the stove, stirring the caramelized vegetables into the soup. The richly aromatic steam rises into the air and I am breathing the spirit of love and healing.

GOLDEN
LENTIL SOUP

I THINK EVERY COUNTRY HAS ITS OWN VERSION
OF LENTIL SOUP. THIS IS MY RECIPE TAKEN FROM
THE EASTERN MEDITERRANEAN REGION.
IT'S THICK AND HEARTY, MAKING IT PERFECT
COMFORT FOOD FOR COLD WEATHER MONTHS.

3 tablespoons olive oil
6 celery stalks, cut into 1/2-inch pieces
3 carrots, peeled and cut into 1/2-inch pieces
2 onions, chopped
1 pound dried red lentils
1/4 cup long-grain white rice
12 cups water
1 tablespoon lemon pepper
1 tablespoon seasoned salt
2 teaspoons salt, plus more to taste
1 1/2 teaspoons ground black pepper, plus more to taste
1/2 teaspoon ground cumin (optional)
1/4 cup fresh lemon juice
   Italian parsley sprigs, for garnish

Heat the oil in a very large stockpot over medium-high heat. Add the celery, carrots, and onions. Sauté until the onions are light caramel color, about 10 minutes. Stir in the lentils and rice and the water. Cover and bring to a boil over high heat, about 20 minutes. Reduce the heat to medium-low. Cover and simmer until the lentils are very soft, stirring occasionally, about 25 minutes. Stir in the lemon pepper, seasoned salt, salt, black pepper, and cumin. Simmer uncovered until the flavors blend, the lentils have fallen apart, and the mixture thickens slightly, stirring occasionally, about 20 minutes. Stir in the lemon juice. Season the soup to taste with more salt and pepper, if desired.

Ladle the soup into bowls. Garnish with Italian parsley sprigs and serve.

COOK'S NOTES: As the red lentils cook, they turn golden and literally look pureed. You can find red lentils in most of your Middle Eastern Markets and natural health foods stores, and some supermarkets.

As an alternative or variation to the soup, melt 2 tablespoons of butter in a heavy small saucepan until it begins to foam, then stir in a teaspoon or so of dried mint. Pour the mint mixture into the soup just before serving. It is delicious!

Be careful with the cumin as some people are allergic to it. It also lends very strong flavor and assertive taste, so add it a little at a time, tasting as you go.

The soup keeps well in the refrigerator for 3 days, and can be frozen for 1 week. It actually becomes more flavorful if it's prepared a day in advance and refrigerated. Rewarm it over medium heat, adding more water to thin it to a desired consistency

Serves 10 to 12

PUREE OF BUTTERNUT SQUASH SOUP

WELCOMING AND COLORFUL, THIS SOUP IS INTENSELY FLAVORED AND TERRIFIC AS A HOLIDAY PARTY FIRST COURSE. FOLLOW IT UP WITH A MIXED BABY GREENS SALAD AND THE DELICIOUS ROASTED RACK OF LAMB WITH POMEGRANATE SAUCE (PAGE 155) OR ROAST PORK RACK WITH SOUR CHERRY SAUCE (PAGE 152). FOR A LIGHT SUPPER, SERVE THE SOUP WITH THE ROSEMARY-PARMESAN SCONES (PAGE 227) – THEY MAKE A PERFECT PAIR!

1 tablespoon unsalted butter, melted
1 large butternut squash (about 2 pounds), halved and seeded
3 tablespoons olive oil
1 large onion, chopped
1 leek (white and pale green parts only), trimmed and thinly sliced
6 garlic cloves, chopped
1 (1-inch) piece fresh ginger, peeled and finely chopped
1 pound yams, peeled and coarsely chopped
5 3/4 cups chicken broth
1 cup whole milk
3 tablespoons pure maple syrup
2 teaspoons salt
1 1/2 teaspoons sugar
1 teaspoon grated orange peel (optional)
1/2 teaspoon ground black pepper
1/4 teaspoon ground cinnamon
1/4 cup (1/2 stick) unsalted butter, room temperature
  Toasted pumpkin seeds, for garnish
  Fresh chive, for garnish

Preheat the oven to 375°F. Brush the melted butter over the cut sides of the squash. Wrap each squash half in foil and place them on a heavy baking sheet. Roast in the oven until the squash is tender, turning occasionally, about 1 hour. Set aside until cool enough to handle. Spoon the flesh into a medium bowl. Discard the skins.

Meanwhile, heat the oil in a heavy large pot over medium-high heat. Add the onion, leek, garlic, and ginger. Sauté until the vegetables are tender, about 5 minutes. Add the yams, the broth and milk. Cover and bring to a boil. Reduce the heat to medium-low. Cover and simmer until the yams are very tender, stirring occasionally, about 30 minutes. Stir in the roasted squash flesh, maple syrup, salt, sugar, orange peel, pepper, and cinnamon. Cool the soup slightly.

Using a hand-held immersion blender, puree the soup in the pot until smooth. Alternately, working in batches, puree the soup in a regular blender or food processor until smooth, then return it to the pot. Add the butter to the soup and whisk over medium heat until the butter melts and the soup is hot.

Ladle the soup into a heated tureen or into individual bowls. Sprinkle with the pumpkin seeds, garnish with the chives, and serve.

COOK'S NOTES: Butternut squash is widely available and will yield a slightly sweet flavor, but any winter squash, such as kabocha, hubbard, acorn squash, or even pumpkin will do.

Using a hand-held immersion blender makes pureeing the soup very easy. Not only does it eliminate the need to transfer the hot soup from the pot to the blender, but since everything is pureed right in the pot there is less to clean. Be careful when pureeing the soup in a regular blender. To prevent any messy splatters, cool the soup slightly before pureeing it, then fill the blender just halfway with the soup. Cover the blender with the lid and drape a thick kitchen towel over the lid to absorb any hot soup that may overflow.

The soup tends to get thicker and even more delicious the next day. You can add milk, water or stock to thin it starting with 1/2 cup at a time. Keep it covered and refrigerated up to 3 days. Bring it to a simmer in a pot over medium heat before serving.

Serves 8 to 10

GAZPACHO

ORIGINALLY FROM SPAIN, THIS TANTALIZING CHILLED SUMMER SOUP IS VERY HEALTHY AND EASY TO PREPARE. IT IS WONDERFUL SUMMERTIME PARTY FARE, ESPECIALLY SINCE THE VEGETABLES CAN BE CHOPPED THE DAY BEFORE, AND THE SOUP CAN BE MADE UP TO EIGHT HOURS AHEAD. I LIKE TO SERVE IT IN COCKTAIL, MARTINI, OR PARFAIT GLASSES WITH LEMON WEDGES AND SHRIMP.

Stir all of the ingredients except the yogurt and celery stalks in a large bowl and stir to mix well. Cover and refrigerate until the soup is very cold, at least 2 hours and up to 8 hours.

Ladle the soup into bowls. Spoon a dollop of plain yogurt or sour cream atop each serving. Garnish with the celery stalks and serve.

COOK'S NOTES: Try the cold soup as a topping for grilled fish or chicken, or on a baked potato as a healthy, low-calorie alternative to butter and sour cream. This soup can also be pureed into a deliciously smooth texture.

Serves 8 to 10

5 3/4 cups vegetable juice
1 hothouse cucumber, seeded and finely diced
3 plum tomatoes, seeded and finely diced
1 small red onion, finely diced
1 green bell pepper, seeded and finely diced
1 red bell pepper, seeded and finely diced
1 yellow bell pepper, seeded and finely diced
2 celery stalks, finely diced
1/2 cup chopped fresh cilantro
1/2 cup chopped fresh mint
1/2 cup finely chopped green onions
1/4 cup red wine vinegar
3 tablespoons fresh lime juice
1/4 fresh lemon juice
1 serrano chili, finely diced (optional)
2 teaspoons salt
1 teaspoon ground black pepper
1 teaspoon seasoned salt
1/2 teaspoon minced garlic
   Plain yogurt or sour cream, for garnish
   Small celery stalks with leaves, for garnish

MEATBALL SOUP
WITH LEMON AND MINT

THIS NATIONAL DISH OF IRAQ, KNOWN
AS *"KOOBA HAMOUD"*, FEATURES AN
AMAZING BALANCE OF TANGY FLAVORS.
EVERYONE MAKES IT DIFFERENTLY,
BUT THIS RECIPE CAPTURES THE
ESSENTIAL QUALITIES OF THE SOUP AS
YOU MIGHT FIND IT IN THE MIDDLE EAST.

Meatballs
2 tablespoons chopped fresh parsley
1 tablespoon chopped fresh mint
1 tablespoon finely chopped garlic
1 1/2 pounds lean ground beef (7% fat)
1 1/2 teaspoons ground black pepper
1 1/2 teaspoons salt
1 cup instant cream of rice
1/2 cup cold water
1 teaspoon paprika

Broth
6 tablespoons (3/4 stick) unsalted butter
1/4 cup minced fresh garlic
3 tablespoons dried mint, crushed
1/3 cup tomato paste
1/4 cup uncooked long-grain white rice
12 cups chicken broth
3/4 cup fresh lemon juice
  Salt and ground black pepper, to taste

To make the meatballs: Stir the parsley, mint, garlic, half of the ground beef, and 1/2 teaspoon of each black pepper and salt in a large bowl to blend. Set the beef filling aside.

Mix the cream of rice and 1/2 cup of cold water in a food processor just to blend. Let stand for 15 minutes (this will allow the cream of rice to soften slightly). Add the remaining half of ground beef, paprika, and remaining 1 teaspoon of each salt and pepper. Pulse until a ball forms.

Using about 1 1/2 tablespoons of the cream of rice mixture for each meatball, flatten it in the palm of your hand, forming a 3-inch-diameter patty. Using about 1 tablespoon of the beef filling for each meatball, spoon the filling into the center of the patty. Fold the patty by lifting its edges up and over the filling and pinching them together to enclose the filling completely. Pinch off any excess patty. Roll the meatball between the palms of your hands to form a firm and smooth egg-shaped meatball. Arrange the meatballs on a baking sheet. Cover and refrigerate until ready to use.

To make the broth: Melt the butter in a heavy large pot over medium heat until it is golden brown, stirring constantly, about 3 minutes. Stir in the garlic and mint and sauté until fragrant, about 30 seconds. Add the tomato paste and stir for 2 minutes. Stir in the rice, then the broth. Cover and bring the mixture to a boil. Reduce the heat to medium. Cover and simmer until the rice is tender, about 10 minutes. Stir in the lemon juice. Cover and bring the broth to a boil again. Add the meatballs and simmer until they are cooked through, about 10 minutes. Season the broth to taste with salt and pepper.

Ladle the broth and meatballs into bowls and serve.

COOK'S NOTES: When making the meatballs, do not use too much rice mixture to enclose the beef filling, since the key to making terrific meatballs is to form a very thin patty that is just large enough to encase the beef filling.

The meatballs can be made in advance. Store them in an airtight container and refrigerate them for 2 days or freeze them for 1 week. Once the soup is made it will keep for 2 days, covered and refrigerated.

Serves 8

MUSHROOM BARLEY SOUP

TRYING DIFFERENT KINDS OF MUSHROOMS IN THIS SOUP WILL YIELD DIFFERENT AND, INTERESTING RESULTS. ANY MUSHROOMS, HOWEVER, WILL ADD THEIR NATURAL UMAMI – A "SIXTH FLAVOR" FOUND IN SOME FOODS, SUCH AS MUSHROOMS, SOY SAUCE AND SUN-DRIED TOMATOES, THAT ENHANCES OTHER FLAVORS.

3 tablespoons olive oil
1 large onion, chopped
3 celery stalks, chopped
1 large carrot, peeled and chopped
1 pound assorted fresh mushrooms, sliced
1 tablespoon chopped fresh oregano
1 tablespoon minced garlic
1/3 cup tomato paste
1 russet potato, peeled and cut into 1/2-inch pieces
1/2 cup pearl barley
5 cups beef broth
2 cups chicken broth
1 1/2 teaspoons seasoned salt
1/2 teaspoon cayenne pepper (optional)
  Oregano sprigs, for garnish

Heat the oil in a heavy large pot over medium-high heat. Add the onion, celery, and carrot. Sauté until the onion is translucent, about 10 minutes. Add the mushrooms, oregano, and garlic. Cook until the liquid evaporates and the mushrooms are tender, stirring frequently, about 15 minutes. Add the tomato paste and stir for 1 minute. Add the potato, barley , and the beef broth and chicken broth. Cover and bring to a boil over high heat, about 15 minutes. Reduce the heat to medium-low. Simmer gently uncovered until the vegetables are tender and the soup thickens slightly, stirring occasionally, about 45 minutes. Stir in the seasoned salt and cayenne pepper. Spoon off any oil that rises to the top of the soup.

Ladle the soup into bowls. Garnish with oregano sprigs and serve.

COOK'S NOTES: Adding coarsely chopped fresh spinach or Swiss chard gives this flavorful soup even more character.

The soup can be made in advance, if desired. Keep it covered and refrigerated up to 2 days, or freeze it up to 1 week. Bring the soup to a simmer in a pot over medium heat before serving.

Serves 6 to 8

COLD CUCUMBER-MINT
SOUP WITH YOGURT

HOSTING A SMALL LUNCHEON OR PARTY ON A HOT SUMMER AFTERNOON? TRY SERVING THIS EASY, HEALTHY TREAT IN PARFAIT GLASSES, GARNISHED WITH MINT AND DICED TOMATOES. YOU CAN MAKE IT A BIT THICKER, BY OMITTING THE WATER AND SERVE IT AS A DIP OR PITA POCKET SPREAD.

4 cups plain yogurt

4 teaspoons crushed dried mint

2 1/4 pounds hothouse cucumbers (about 2 or 3), seeded and finely diced

1/4 cup coarsely chopped fresh mint

2 ripe tomatoes, seeded and finely diced

1 1/2 cups very cold water

2 1/2 teaspoons salt

1 garlic clove, minced

Ice cubes

Fresh mint sprigs, for garnish

Whisk the yogurt and dried mint in a large bowl until creamy. Stir in the cucumbers and the chopped fresh mint. Add all but 1/2 cup of the tomatoes. Whisk in the cold water, salt and garlic. Cover and refrigerate until the soup is very cold, stirring occasionally to help blend the flavors, at least 1 hour or up to 1 day.

Ladle the soup into a large glass bowl and stir in the ice cubes to keep it cool. Or ladle the soup into individual bowls, adding two large or three small ice cubes to each. Garnish with the remaining 1/2 cup of tomatoes and mint sprigs, and serve.

COOK'S NOTES: The traditional way of serving this soup is without tomatoes, but I find they add a wonderfully sweet dimension to the soup, and contrasting color. I also prefer using hothouse cucumbers because they're virtually seedless with tender, mild skins that add color to the soup. Japanese cucumbers, which are similar to hothouse cucumbers but smaller, work well, too. Of course, you can use regular cucumbers, but you'll need to peel them first.

Experiment by adding other ingredients to this recipe. For instance, mound fresh cooked crabmeat or bay shrimp atop the soup. Cooked barley also makes a fabulous addition to this soup. Just add about 1 cup of cold cooked barley along with the cucumbers.

Serves 6 to 8

GREEN LENTIL SOUP
WITH SWISS CHARD

THIS HEALTHY SOUP IS SATISFYING IN SO
MANY WAYS; IT'S NOURISHING, COMFORTING,
DELICIOUS, AND COLORFUL. AND THE
COMBINATION OF RICE, LENTILS, AND BEANS
MAKES IT A HEARTY MEAL IN ITSELF. SERVE
IT WITH CRUSTY BREAD AND A GLASS OF RED
WINE FOR A SIMPLE BUT FABULOUS SUPPER.

1/2 cup olive oil
3 medium onions, chopped
8 celery stalks, chopped
1 (6-ounce) can tomato paste
1/4 cup minced garlic
1 1/2 cups dried green lentils
1/4 cup uncooked short-grain white rice
  (such as arborio or pearl rice)
1 bunch red Swiss chard, leaves and
  stems coarsely chopped
2 medium russet potatoes, peeled and
  cut into 1/2-inch pieces
4 plum tomatoes, seeded and chopped
12 cups chicken broth or water
1 (15 1/2-ounce) can garbanzo beans,
  rinsed and drained
1 tablespoon salt, plus more to taste
1 teaspoon ground black pepper, plus more to taste
1 teaspoon seasoned salt
1/2 teaspoon dried crushed red pepper
1/3 cup fresh lemon juice
  Lemon wedges, for garnish
  Parsley sprigs, for garnish

Heat the oil in an 8-quart stockpot over medium-high
heat. Add the onions and celery. Sauté until the onions
are translucent, about 10 minutes. Add the tomato
paste and garlic, and stir for 1 minute. Stir in the
lentils and rice, then the chard, potatoes, and tomatoes.
Add the broth. Cover and bring to a boil over high
heat, about 20 minutes. Reduce the heat to medium-
low. Cover and simmer until the flavors blend and
the potatoes are tender, stirring occasionally, about
25 minutes. Stir in the garbanzo beans, 1 tablespoon
of salt, 1 teaspoon of black pepper, seasoned salt, and
crushed red pepper. Simmer until the beans are heated
through and the flavors blend, about 10 minutes.
Stir in the lemon juice. Season the soup with more
salt and pepper, if desired.

Ladle the soup into bowls. Garnish with lemon wedges
and parsley sprigs, and serve

COOK'S NOTES: Swiss chard lends a unique flavor, which
really makes a big difference in this soup. There are
many ways to vary this recipe to suit seasonal produce
or particular palates. Try adding fresh vegetables such
as green beans, mushrooms, or zucchini. Black beans
or white beans make good substitutes for the garbanzo
beans, and pearl barley works well in place of the rice.
For a heartier meal add cooked chicken sausage when
adding the beans.

This recipe makes a nice large stockpot of soup. Since it
freezes very well, eat some now and save some for later.
Keep it covered and refrigerated up to 2 days, or freeze
it up to 1 week. Bring the soup to a simmer in a pot over
medium heat before serving.

Serves 12 to 14

MANTI

MANTI IS A DISH ORIGINATING FROM CENTRAL ASIA. IT IS COMPRISED OF SMALL DUMPLINGS FILLED WITH SPICY GROUND BEEF OR LAMB SERVED IN A FLAVORFUL BROTH. SUBTLY EXOTIC, THE DISH WORKS WELL AS EITHER A UNIQUE APPETIZER OR A HEARTY MAIN DISH. THE TRICK IS TO ROLL THE DOUGH AS THIN AS POSSIBLE, A SKILL THAT REQUIRES PATIENCE AND PRACTICE. IF YOU HAVE A LITTLE EXTRA TIME TO DEDICATE TO THAT TASK, YOU'LL FIND IT'S WELL WORTH IT. IF YOU DON'T HAVE A LOT OF TIME, GO AHEAD AND USE PRE-MADE WON TON SKINS INSTEAD OF MAKING THE DOUGH FROM SCRATCH.

Dumplings

2 cups all purpose flour, plus more for dusting
1 3/4 teaspoons salt
2/3 cup water
1 pound lean ground beef (7% fat)
1/2 cup chopped fresh parsley
1/2 cup finely chopped onion
3/4 teaspoon garlic powder
3/4 teaspoon ground black pepper
3/4 teaspoon lemon pepper
2 tablespoons (1/4 stick) unsalted butter, melted

Soup

1/2 cup (1 stick) unsalted butter
3 tablespoons dried mint, crushed
3 tablespoons minced garlic
8 cups chicken broth
1/2 teaspoon salt, plus more to taste
1/2 cup yogurt cheese (page 14) or plain yogurt

To make the dumplings: Lightly flour a baking sheet. Combine 2 cups of flour and 3/4 teaspoon of salt in a food processor. With the machine running, add the water through the feed tube and blend just until the dough forms. Gather the dough into a ball and transfer it to a floured work surface. Knead just until smooth and elastic, about 1 minute. Divide the dough into 3 equal pieces. Arrange the dough on the prepared baking sheet. Cover with plastic wrap and let stand for 30 minutes (this will relax the dough and allow it to stretch more easily).

Meanwhile, mix the beef, parsley, onion, garlic powder, black pepper, lemon pepper, and the remaining 1 teaspoon of salt in a medium bowl to blend.

Preheat the oven to 450°F. Line a baking sheet with parchment paper. Working with 1 piece of dough at a time, roll out the dough on a lightly floured work surface into a very thin 13-inch-diameter round. Cut the dough into 1 1/2-inch squares. Place 1/2 teaspoon of the beef mixture in the center of each square. Fold up 2 sides of each square of dough to encase the beef mixture but not enclose it. Pinch the ends of the dough square to seal. Arrange the dumplings on the prepared baking sheet. Brush the melted butter over the tops of the dumplings.

Bake until the dumplings are golden brown on the bottom and around the edges, and the filling is cooked through, about 8 minutes. Set aside and keep warm.

To make the soup: Melt the butter in a heavy large pot over medium heat until it is golden brown, stirring constantly, about 3 minutes. Stir in the mint and garlic and sauté until fragrant, about 30 seconds. Add the broth and 1/2 teaspoon of salt. Bring the broth to a boil. Season to taste with more salt, if desired.

Place about 20 warm dumplings in each bowl. Ladle the hot broth over. Spoon a dollop of yogurt atop each and serve.

COOK'S NOTES: The dumplings can be made in advance. Once they are baked, cool them completely, then enclose them in an airtight container and refrigerate for 2 days or freeze up to 2 weeks. Just before serving, arrange them on a baking sheet and rewarm them in a 350°F oven, until just heated through.

Serves 8 to 10

VINE-RIPENED ROASTED TOMATO-BASIL SOUP

SERVE THIS SOUP WITH WARM SESAME RING ROLLS (PAGE 242) OR WITH TOASTED FRENCH BREAD SLICES SPRINKLED WITH FRESHLY GRATED PARMESAN CHEESE.

3 tablespoons plus 1/3 cup olive oil
2 tablespoons plus 1/2 cup thinly sliced fresh basil
4 tablespoons minced garlic
2 1/2 teaspoons ground black pepper
1 teaspoon plus 1 tablespoon salt
10 plum tomatoes, halved lengthwise
2 onions, chopped
3 large leeks (white and pale green parts only), sliced
4 celery stalks, chopped
1/3 cup tomato paste
8 cups chicken broth
2 medium russet potatoes, peeled and
   cut into 1/2-inch pieces
3 tablespoons chopped fresh thyme
2 tablespoons unsalted butter (optional)
   Basil sprigs, for garnish

Preheat the oven to 475°F. Line a heavy baking sheet with parchment paper or aluminum foil. Whisk 3 tablespoons of oil, 2 tablespoons of basil, 2 tablespoons of garlic, and 1 teaspoon each of black pepper and salt in a large bowl. Add the tomato halves and toss to coat. Place the tomatoes, cut side up, on the prepared baking sheet. Spoon any remaining oil mixture over the tomatoes. Bake until the skins loosen from the tomatoes, about 10 minutes. Set the tomatoes aside until they are cool enough to handle. Peel and coarsely chop the tomatoes, and transfer them with their juices to a medium bowl. Set aside.

Heat the remaining 1/3 cup of oil in a heavy large pot over medium-high heat. Add the onions, leeks, and celery, and sauté until they are translucent, about 10 minutes. Add the tomato paste and remaining 2 tablespoons of garlic and stir for 1 minute. Add the roasted tomatoes and any accumulated juices from the baking sheet, the broth, potatoes, thyme, and remaining 1/2 cup of basil. Bring the soup to a boil. Reduce the heat to medium-low. Cover and simmer until the vegetables are tender, stirring occasionally, about 35 minutes. Stir in the butter, and remaining 1 1/2 teaspoons of black pepper and 1 tablespoon of salt.

Ladle the soup into bowls. Garnish with basil sprigs, and serve.

COOK'S NOTES: In order to get the most out of this delicious soup, make sure your tomatoes are red and ripe, but still slightly firm to the touch.

This soup is best served the day it is made, but it will keep up to 2 days, covered and refrigerated. Bring the soup to a simmer in a pot over medium heat before serving.

Serves 8 to 10

ROASTED TOMATO AND EGGPLANT SOUP

THIS RECIPE DOES TAKE A LITTLE EXTRA
TIME, BUT YOU'LL FIND IT IS WELL WORTH IT.
THE SMOKY FLAVORS FROM ROASTING THE
EGGPLANT AND BELL PEPPERS ARE THE SECRET
OF THE DELICIOUS RESULTS. SERVE IT WITH
SOU BOREG (PAGE 130), CRUSTY FRENCH BREAD,
A SIMPLE SIDE SALAD, OR THE SPINACH
SALAD WITH SMOKED TURKEY (PAGE 87).

1 large eggplant (about 1 1/2 pounds)
4 tablespoons chopped fresh basil
3 tablespoons olive oil
2 teaspoons plus 2 tablespoons minced garlic
1 1/2 teaspoons salt, plus more to taste
1 teaspoon ground black pepper, plus more to taste
3 plum tomatoes, halved lengthwise
3 red bell peppers
1 onion, chopped
1 leek (white and pale green parts only), thinly sliced
2 tablespoons tomato paste
4 1/4 cups chicken broth
1 tablespoon fresh thyme leaves, chopped
2 teaspoons seasoned salt
2 tablespoons fresh lemon juice
2 tablespoons unsalted butter
  Shaved Parmesan cheese, for garnish

Preheat the oven to 475°F. Line 2 heavy baking sheets with parchment paper or aluminum foil. Pierce the eggplant with a knife in several places. Place it on 1 baking sheet. Roast until the eggplant is charred on the outside and very tender inside, turning occasionally, about 40 minutes. Set the eggplant aside until cool enough to handle. Cut the eggplants lengthwise in half. Scraping as close to the eggplant skins as possible, spoon the soft pulp into a medium bowl. Discard the skins.

Whisk 1 tablespoon of basil, 1 tablespoon of oil, 2 teaspoons of garlic, and 1/2 teaspoon each of salt and pepper in a medium bowl. Add the tomato halves and toss to coat. Place the tomatoes, cut side up, on the second prepared baking sheet. Spoon any remaining oil mixture over the tomatoes. Bake just until the skins loosen from the tomatoes (do not overcook), about 10 minutes. Set aside until the tomatoes are cool enough to handle. Peel the tomatoes, then transfer them to the bowl with the eggplant.

Meanwhile, char the red bell peppers over a gas flame or under the broiler until blackened on all sides, about 10 minutes. Enclose the peppers in a plastic bag for 10 minutes. Peel, seed and coarsely chop the peppers. Transfer the peppers to the eggplant mixture.

Heat the remaining 2 tablespoons of oil in a large pot over medium-high heat. Add the onion and leek, and sauté until they are translucent, about 8 minutes. Add the remaining 2 tablespoons garlic and sauté for 1 minute. Stir in tomato paste and eggplant mixture. Add the broth. Bring the mixture to a boil. Reduce the heat to medium-low. Cover and simmer until the vegetables are very tender, stirring occasionally, about 35 minutes. Stir in the thyme, seasoned salt, and remaining 3 tablespoons of basil, 1 teaspoon of salt, and 1/2 teaspoon of black pepper. Set the soup aside to cool slightly.

Using a hand-held immersion blender, puree the soup in the pot until smooth. Alternately, working in batches, puree the soup in a regular blender or food processor until smooth, then return it to the pot. Add the lemon juice and butter. Stir over low heat until the soup is hot. Season the soup to taste with more salt and pepper, if desired.

Ladle the soup into bowls. Sprinkle with the Parmesan cheese and serve.

COOK'S NOTES: : Make sure the eggplant is cooked thoroughly. If it's not cooked all the way through, it will taste quite bitter.

Using a hand-held immersion blender makes pureeing the soup very easy. Not only does it eliminate the need to transfer the hot soup from the pot to the blender, but since everything is pureed right in the pot there is less to clean. Be careful when pureeing the soup in a regular blender. To prevent any messy splatters, cool the soup slightly before pureeing it, then fill the blender just halfway with the soup. Cover the blender with the lid and drape a thick kitchen towel over the lid to absorb any hot soup that may overflow.

This soup will keep for 3 days, covered and refrigerated. Bring it to a simmer in a pot over medium heat before serving.

Serves 6 to 8

WHITE BEAN SOUP WITH SAGE

SERVE THIS DELICIOUS HEARTY SOUP WITH TOASTED GARLIC-RUBBED CROSTINI, BREADSTICKS, OR ROSEMARY-PARMESAN SCONES (PAGE 227), AND THE ROMAINE SALAD WITH HEARTS OF PALM, AND ARTICHOKES (PAGE 64).

1/2 cup olive oil
2 large onions, chopped
1 leek (white and pale green parts only), thinly sliced
2 celery stalks, thinly sliced
1 large carrot, peeled and thinly sliced
6 garlic cloves, minced
3 tablespoons chopped fresh Italian parsley
3 tablespoons chopped fresh sage
1 (6-ounce) can tomato paste
6 cups chicken broth
3 cups hot water
2 cups dried great Northern white beans
4 plum tomatoes, seeded and diced
1 tablespoon salt
1 teaspoon ground black pepper
1/8 teaspoon dried crushed red pepper (optional)
  Extra-virgin olive oil, for garnish
  Small sage leaves, for garnish

Heat the olive oil in a heavy large pot over medium-high heat. Add the onions, leek, celery, carrot, and garlic, and sauté until the vegetables are tender, about 10 minutes. Add the parsley and sage and sauté for 1 minute. Stir in the tomato paste. Add the broth and 3 cups of hot water. Stir in the beans and tomatoes. Bring the mixture to a boil. Reduce the heat to medium-low. Cover and simmer gently until the beans are soft, stirring occasionally, about 2 hours. Add the salt, black pepper, and crushed red pepper.

Ladle the soup into bowls. Drizzle 1/2 teaspoon of extra-virgin olive oil over each serving. Garnish with sage leaves, and serve.

COOK'S NOTES: This is a good basic soup for adding all sorts of your favorite vegetables. I like it with jicama, potatoes, spinach, or Swiss chard. I also like to sprinkle freshly grated Parmesan cheese and crunchy croutons over the soup just before serving for a wonderful textural contrast.

As a rule of thumb, one cup of dried beans yields about 3 cups when cooked. It's important to simmer the soup on medium-low heat. Boiling the beans on high heat will cause the skins to separate. Also, don't season the soup with salt until after the beans are cook and tender. Salt tends to toughen the beans if added to soon.

Serves 6 to 8

VEGETABLES

ASTAS GRAINS

This chapter will encourage daring by the cook and includes traditional as well as innovative recipes for mostly vegetarian dishes. A favorite of mine is my mother's classic Sou Boreg—a jewel of a dish that evokes strong, sweet memories of holiday meals with my family

KESSAB, SYRIA 1955

One of my most vivid memories of my mother's homeland, Kessab, Syria, is of my grandmother preparing one of my favorite foods: cheese.

When I was very young, my grandmother—a short woman with soft white hair pulled back into a bun—was already in her 80's. Her angelic features and fair skin contrasted sharply with her dark dresses. I recall her seriousness as she cut blocks of firm goat cheese into cubes, salted them, and packed them into narrow-necked vessels of red pottery. She covered the tops with gauze and sealed them with soft clay. I followed her into the front yard and watched her bend near shallow holes in the ground. Carefully, grandmother turned the jars upside down, lowered them in, and refilled the holes, burying the cheese for almost 12 months. This was the traditional method of aging goat cheese, a tradition she learned from her mother that had been passed down through ages.

When the cheese was ready, grandmother would return to the yard. I recall watching her squat over the holes, slowly fighting the earth to resurrect the vessels. Gradually the pots emerged. She removed the soft clay seals, the white gauze, then the cheese—now cool and pungent with saltiness. She served it with warm, soft flat bread—a delightful contrast to the tangy, crumbly cheese (similar to bleu cheese, without the vein).To this day, the flavor and texture of the cheese and bread linger in my memory. Many of my favorite recipes feature cheese as a key ingredient.

Take, for instance, the wonderful Mediterranean twist on traditional angel hair pasta featured on page 124. The slight bite of feta cheese contrasts enticingly with the smoky crunch of toasted pine nuts and the fruitiness of fresh plum tomatoes. The firm capellini strands tangle these flavors with the zip of garlic, the tart of bright green parsley, and the saltiness of Parmesan cheese so that every bite is a rich ensemble of exciting flavor.

ANGEL HAIR PASTA WITH TOMATOES, FETA, AND PINE NUTS

WHEN I FIRST OPENED MY RESTAURANT, "ANGEL HAIR" WAS THE ITALIAN BUZZWORD FOR PASTA DISHES. I ADDED FETA CHEESE TO FRESH TOMATOES AND BASIL, AND THIS LIGHT, MEDITERRANEAN; ANGEL HAIR PASTA DISH WAS BORN! IT QUICKLY BECAME ONE OF OUR SIGNATURE DISHES AND A FAVORITE AMONG OUR CUSTOMERS.

8 ounces dried angel hair or capellini pasta
1 tablespoon plus 1/3 cup olive oil
1/2 cup thinly sliced fresh basil
3 tablespoons chopped fresh Italian parsley
2 tablespoons minced garlic
2 tablespoons minced shallots
1 1/2 pounds plum tomatoes, diced
1 teaspoon salt
3/4 teaspoon ground black pepper
1 cup coarsely crumbled feta cheese
1/2 cup freshly shredded Parmesan cheese
1/3 cup pine nuts, toasted (page 18)
1/4 cup shaved Parmesan cheese

Bring a large pot of salted water to a boil over high heat. Stir in the pasta and cook for just 1 minute (this is to soften the pasta slightly). Drain the pasta in a colander, reserving 1/4 cup of the cooking liquid. Toss the hot pasta in a large bowl with 1 tablespoon of oil to prevent it from sticking together. Set the pasta and reserved cooking liquid aside.

Heat the remaining 1/3 cup of oil in a deep large nonstick frying pan over high heat. Add the basil, parsley, garlic, and shallots. Stir just until fragrant, about 20 seconds. Add the tomatoes and sauté just until they are heated through, about 45 seconds. Remove the skillet from the heat. Stir in the salt and black pepper. Stir in the feta cheese and the shredded Parmesan cheese. Add the pasta and toss gently to combine, adding some of the reserved cooking liquid to moisten, if necessary.

Mound the pasta on a large platter or atop individual plates. Sprinkle the pine nuts and shaved Parmesan cheese over, and serve immediately.

COOK'S NOTES: Experiment by using different tomatoes. Grape tomatoes, teardrop tomatoes and cherry tomatoes make wonderful substitutes for the plum tomatoes. Make sure not to overcook the tomatoes, as they should be just barely warm when tossed with the other ingredients.

Serves 4 to 6

BULGUR PILAF WITH GARBANZO BEANS AND TOASTED PITA

BULGUR IS SUBTLE ENOUGH THAT IT PICKS UP OTHER FLAVORS, WHICH IS WHY I ALSO LOVE TO SERVE IT WITH FISH OR CHICKEN KEBABS AND DOLLOPS OF MINT-FLAVORED YOGURT.

1 1/4 sticks unsalted butter
1 pita bread, halved horizontally,
  cut into 1/4-inch matchstick-size strips
2 cups coarse bulgur (#4 grade) (page 12)
1 teaspoon salt
1/2 teaspoon ground black pepper
3 1/2 cups chicken broth
1 (15 1/2 ounce) can garbanzo beans,
  rinsed and drained

Melt the butter in a heavy large saucepan over medium heat. Add the pita strips, and sauté until they are brown and crisp, about 6 minutes. Remove the pan from the heat. Using a meshed or slotted spoon, transfer the toasted pita pieces and strips to a plate and set them aside.

Return the pan to the heat. Stir in the bulgur, salt, and pepper. Sauté for 1 minute. Stir in the broth and beans. Increase the heat to high and bring the broth to a simmer. Decrease the heat to low. Cover and simmer until the bulgur is tender and the broth is absorbed, about 25 minutes (do not stir the bulgur while it cooks). Remove the pan from the heat. Uncover and let the pilaf stand for 2 minutes to allow any remaining steam to dissipate.

Transfer the pilaf to a serving bowl. Add three-fourths of the toasted pita pieces and strips. Using a large fork, fluff the pilaf while mixing in the toasted pita. Sprinkle the remaining toasted pita atop the pilaf and serve.

COOK'S NOTES: For variation, try adding 1 cup of sautéed mushrooms, peas, or corn for a colorful dish. If you're a walnut fan, I highly suggest garnishing the dish with chopped toasted walnuts.

Serves 6 to 8

SPINACH AND LEEK SPANAKOPITA

THE RICOTTA CHEESE ADDS A NICE CREAMY TEXTURE TO THE SPINACH AND LEEK FILLING THAT CONTRASTS WELL WITH THE DELICATE LAYERS OF CRISP, FLAKY PHYLLO DOUGH. TRADITIONALLY, THIS DISH IS SERVED AT SPECIAL OCCASIONS ON A BUFFET TABLE ALONG WITH SEVERAL MAIN ENTREES.

2 1/2 pounds cleaned spinach,
  stems removed (not baby)
1 teaspoon salt
1 tablespoon olive oil
3/4 cup (1 1/2 sticks) unsalted butter
3 leeks (white and pale green parts only), thinly sliced
1/2 cup minced shallots
4 teaspoons minced garlic
1/2 cup whipping cream
4 large eggs
2 tablespoons chopped fresh dill
1 1/2 teaspoons ground black pepper
1 teaspoon seasoned salt
1 cup low-fat ricotta cheese
8 ounces feta cheese, crumbled
16 frozen phyllo pastry sheets, thawed

Heat a heavy large skillet over medium-high heat. Working in two batches, add the spinach and 1/4 teaspoon of salt and sauté until the spinach wilts, about 1 minute and 30 seconds. Transfer the spinach to a colander to drain and cool. Squeeze the spinach to remove any excess water. Set the spinach aside.

Heat the oil and 2 tablespoons of butter in the same large skillet over medium heat. Add the leeks and sauté until wilted, about 3 minutes. Add the shallots and garlic and sauté until they are tender and translucent, about 5 minutes. Set aside to cool.

Whisk the cream, eggs, dill, pepper, seasoned salt, and remaining 1/2 teaspoon of salt in a large bowl to blend. Stir in the spinach and leek mixtures, then the ricotta cheese and feta cheese.

Preheat the oven to 350°F. Melt the remaining butter in a small saucepan. Brush some of the melted butter over a 13x9x2-inch baking dish. Unroll the phyllo sheets on a smooth, flat, dry surface. Carefully remove 1 sheet of phyllo and lay half of it over the bottom of the baking dish (keep the remaining phyllo sheets covered with plastic wrap and a damp kitchen towel). Brush some butter over the phyllo sheet in the dish. Fold the overhanging half of the phyllo sheet atop the sheet in the dish. Brush the top sheet with some butter. Repeat with 7 more phyllo sheets, brushing each with butter. Spread the spinach mixture evenly over the buttered phyllo sheets. Repeat layering the remaining 8 phyllo sheets atop the spinach mixture, brushing each with butter. Using a sharp knife, make 5 diagonal cuts across the phyllo, cutting through the top layers only and spacing the cuts evenly apart. Repeat in the opposite direction to form a diamond pattern. Bake until the top is amber brown and the phyllo layers are baked through, about 1 hour and 20 minutes. Allow the spanakopita to cool slightly for 10 minutes before serving.

COOK'S NOTES: Use an attractive baking dish that can go from the oven to the table for this beautiful savory pastry. If you don't have a rectangular baking dish, use a large oval or round baking dish instead.

The spanakopita can be made in advance. Cover and refrigerate it up to 2 days, or freeze it up to 1 week. To serve, thaw it if necessary, then cover it very loosely with foil and bake it in a 350°F oven until it is heated through, about 30 minutes.

Serves 10 to 12

SOU-BOREG, LAYERED PASTA WITH MONTEREY JACK CHEESE

NO LAYERED HOMEMADE PASTA COULD BE MORE ELEGANT, AND NONE TASTIER THAN SOU-BOREG. THE DELICIOUS TENDER THIN LAYERS OF PASTA ARE STACKED HIGH AND OOZE MELTING CHEESE WITH EACH BITE – WITH ONE BITE YOU'RE TRANSPORTED TO HEAVEN. MY MOTHER HAS BEEN MAKING SOU-BOREG FOR DECADES. THIS CELEBRATORY DISH IS BASICALLY A SIMPLE COMPOSITION OF INGREDIENTS THAT EVOKES THE SPIRIT OF THE HOLIDAY SEASON. IT SEEMS COMPLICATED TO PREPARE BUT THE PROCEDURE IS LIKE MAKING LASAGNA.

3 1/4 cups all purpose flour, plus more for dusting
5 large eggs
4 teaspoons plus 3 tablespoons salt
1 pound Monterey Jack cheese, shredded
3/4 cup chopped Italian parsley
3/4 cup (1 1/2 sticks) butter, melted

Lightly flour a baking sheet. Blend the eggs and 4 teaspoons of salt in a food processor. Add 3 1/4 cups of flour and blend just until the dough forms. Gather the dough into a ball and transfer it to a floured work surface. Knead just until smooth and elastic, about 1 minute. Divide the dough into 7 equal pieces (about 3 1/2 ounces each), and shape into balls. Arrange the dough balls on the prepared baking sheet. Dust the tops with flour. Cover with plastic wrap and refrigerate at least 3 hours or up to 1 day (this will relax the dough and allow it to stretch more easily).

Meanwhile, toss the cheese and parsley in a medium bowl to combine. Cover and refrigerate until ready to use.

Working with one piece of dough at a time, roll out the dough on a lightly floured work surface into very thin 17x12-inch rectangles. Stack the pasta sheets on a large baking sheet, dusting each with flour to prevent them from sticking together.

Fill a large roasting pan halfway with water. Add the remaining 3 tablespoons of salt and bring the water to a boil over high heat. Prepare a large bowl of ice water. Lay a large clean kitchen towel on the work surface. Working with 1 pasta sheet at a time, submerge the sheet into the boiling salted water and cook for 30 seconds, keeping the sheet as flat as possible. Using tongs, carefully transfer the pasta sheet to the ice water to cool completely, unfolding any creases and smoothing the surface. Remove the pasta sheet from the ice water and pat dry with the towel. Place the pasta sheet on a piece of plastic wrap. Top with piece of plastic wrap. Repeat with the remaining pasta sheets.

Preheat the oven to 350°F. Generously butter a 13x9x2-inch baking dish. Line the baking dish with 1 pasta sheet. Generously butter the pasta sheet. Ruffle the sheet to fit it into the bottom of the dish. Repeat with two more pasta sheets and butter. Top with a fourth pasta sheet, allowing it to hang over the sides of the dish. Sprinkle the cheese mixture over the pasta sheet then fold the overhanging sheet over the cheese mixture (it will not cover the cheese mixture completely). Brush the top of the folded pasta sheet with butter. Repeat layering and buttering the remaining 3 pasta sheets. Cut the sou-boreg into 8 or 12 equal pieces.

Bake until the cheese melts and the top is golden, about 45 minutes. Let stand 10 minutes to cool slightly, then serve.

COOK'S NOTES: The sou-boreg can be assembled up to one month in advance, then covered well and frozen. Be sure to cut the sou-boreg into 8 to 12 equal pieces before baking it.

Nothing beats the fresh homemade pasta sheets in this dish. But if you're short on time, you may substitute them with purchased fresh lasagna sheets, which are available in the refrigerator section of some specialty foods stores. Just be sure they are very, very thin.

Serves 8 to 12

CLASSIC
RICE PILAF

THIS BASIC RICE PILAF IS SUCH A GREAT SIDE DISH TO SO MANY GRILLED AND ROASTED MEATS AND FISH, THAT IT MAY SOON BECOME A STAPLE IN YOUR KITCHEN AS IT IS IN MINE. BUT DON'T LIMIT IT TO THE ROLL OF A SIDE DISH. I ALSO LIKE TO USE IT IN THE BEEF STUFFING FOR THE BEEF BRIOUATS (PAGE 42). YOU CAN USE THE LEFTOVER RICE PILAF TO MAKE A WONDERFUL ORIENTAL SALAD BY ADDING CHOPPED CELERY, ONIONS, CILANTRO, MUSHROOMS, SUGAR SNAP PEAS, GINGER, OR WHATEVER VEGETABLES YOU MIGHT HAVE ON HAND, AND TOSSING IT ALL TOGETHER WITH A GARLICKY SOY SAUCE AND TOASTED SESAME OIL DRESSING.

1/2 cup vermicelli or fideo noodles
6 tablespoons (3/4 stick) unsalted butter
1 cup jasmine rice (see Cook's Notes)
1 teaspoon salt
1/2 teaspoon ground black pepper
1 3/4 cups vegetable broth
1/4 cup water

Preheat the oven to 350°F. Arrange the vermicelli on a heavy baking sheet. Bake the vermicelli until they are golden brown, stirring occasionally to ensure even browning, about 5 minutes. Set the vermicelli aside.

Melt the butter in a heavy medium saucepan over medium-low heat. Stir in the rice and toasted vermicelli. Stir in the salt and pepper. Add the broth and water. Increase the heat to high and bring the cooking liquid to a boil. Cover and simmer gently over low heat until the rice is tender and the liquid is absorbed, about 20 minutes (do not stir the rice as it cooks). Remove the saucepan from the heat. Fluff the rice with a large fork. Transfer to a bowl and serve.

COOK'S NOTES: Good pilaf starts with good-quality rice. I love the fragrant aroma of jasmine rice. It works particularly well in pilafs because its long grains resist becoming sticky when cooked. You can find jasmine rice at natural foods stores and some supermarkets, but I recommend purchasing it at Asian markets where it's likely to be fresher, less expensive, and available in bulk. If jasmine rice is unavailable, use basmati rice or another long-grain white rice instead.

For variation, substitute 1 cup of tomato sauce for 1 cup of the vegetable broth to make a Spanish rice. Or, rinse 10 ounces of frozen soybeans, also known as edamame, and add them and 1/4 cup of chopped fresh dill to the rice mixture just before adding the broth. The soybeans do not need to be thawed.

For a buffet, double the recipe and mound the pilaf on a platter and sprinkle with 1/3 cup of each toasted pine nuts, diced dried apricots, golden raisins, and toasted slivered almonds. Unsalted pistachios and dried currants also make good additions.

Serves 4 to 6

NORTHERN CALIFORNIA 1965

At Zov's Bistro, we try to incorporate flavors and fragrances in our dishes that evoke the sense of warm family gatherings. I recall such get-togethers from my childhood, when rain pecked at the roof of our modest house in Northern California -- sounds that could barely be heard from inside. My cousins were there, the children's giggles rising high over the soft classical music filtering through the room from the stereo. Father, in his usual dark-colored suit, reclined deeply into the sofa, his short legs stretched before him. Eyes closed, he would prop his head with one hand and move it back and forth to Handel's Water Music Suite, his favorite composition. In his mind he was conducting the orchestra.

On the far side of the sofa stood my mother, tall and slender, conducting an orchestra of her own—one of flavor, texture and delicious aromas. She held the handle of a large skillet on the stove, bringing oil to a high heat. On the counter next to her, thinly sliced onions were waiting to sizzle. When ready, mother poured them into the pan and caramelized them. She then turned down the heat to cook them slowly, all the while gently stirring the contents. This released into the air the onion's deep sweetness, intoxicating us all.

Caramelized onions are the key ingredient of Medgederah, our family's favorite side dish. Medgederah is a mixture of green lentils and fragrant jasmine rice, woven through with sweet, succulent, caramelized onions. It is humble food, as old as history, savored by peasant and prince alike. At my restaurant, I offer Medgederah as a vegetarian side dish or serve it with salmon and lemon sauce. At home, we stuff Medgederah into pita bread, top with tomato salad, and roll it up like a burrito. So delicious, the dish itself evokes a sense of belonging to a family.

RICE PILAF WITH LENTILS AND CARAMELIZED ONIONS

I GREW UP EATING AND LOVING THIS CLASSIC PILAF WITH LENTILS ALSO CALLED MEDGEDERAH. AND BECAUSE IT'S SO DELICIOUS AND HEALTHFUL, I SERVE IT AT THE RESTAURANT UNDER MIXED BABY GREENS THAT HAVE BEEN TOSSED WITH A LIGHT VINAIGRETTE, AND TOP IT WITH GRILLED SALMON. A SMALL BOWL OF PLAIN YOGURT COMPLEMENTS ALL THE DIFFERENT TEXTURES AND FLAVORS.

1/3 cup vegetable oil
2 large onions, thinly sliced (about 6 cups)
5 3/4 cups water
2 cups dried green lentils
6 tablespoons (3/4 stick) unsalted butter,
 cut into pieces
2 cups long-grain white rice
2 teaspoons salt
1 teaspoon ground black pepper
 Mint sprigs, for garnish

Heat the oil in a deep large nonstick frying pan over medium heat. Add the onions and sauté until they are deep golden brown and caramelized, about 45 minutes. Set aside.

Combine the water and lentils in a heavy large saucepan. Cover and bring the water to a boil over high heat. Decrease the heat to medium-low and simmer gently until the lentils are almost tender, but still firm to the bite, about 5 minutes. Stir in the butter. Add the rice, salt, and pepper. Cover and bring the cooking liquid to a boil again over high heat. Decrease the heat to medium-low and simmer until the rice and lentils are tender and the cooking liquid is absorbed (do not stir the mixture while it cooks), about 20 minutes. If some water remains unabsorbed in the saucepan, remove the saucepan from the heat and let it stand uncovered for 5 minutes.

Fold the caramelized onions into the pilaf. Transfer the pilaf to a bowl. Garnish with mint sprigs and serve.

COOK'S NOTES: This dish is a great side dish and a wonderful companion to grilled salmon or halibut. Top it with crisp fried onion rings for a contrast in texture, or serve it with a simple tomato salad for a fantastic meatless meal.

The pilaf will keep for 2 days, covered and refrigerated. To serve, rewarm it over medium-low heat, fluffing it with a fork to ensure that it warms thoroughly and evenly.

Serves 8 to 10

EGGPLANT TAGINE

IF YOU HAVEN'T COOKED MUCH EGGPLANT IN THE PAST, I ENCOURAGE YOU TO BE COURAGEOUS AND TRY PREPARING DISHES SUCH AS THIS TRULY VERSATILE AND SATISFYING TAGINE. A TAGINE IS A NORTH AFRICAN STEW TRADITIONALLY COOKED IN EARTHENWARE BOWLS WITH CONICAL COVERS. THOUGH THIS IS MY VEGETARIAN VERSION, TAGINES USUALLY FEATURE LAMB, BEEF, FISH, OR CHICKEN, AND DRIED FRUITS SUCH AS APRICOTS OR PRUNES. SUCH FLAVOR COMBINATIONS MAKE FOR UNIQUE DINNER ENTRÉES. SERVE THIS TAGINE WITH STEAMED PLAIN COUSCOUS, OR RICE PILAF (PAGE 133), FOR A VERY SATISFYING VEGETARIAN DINNER, OR AS AN ACCOMPANIMENT TO GRILLED CHICKEN OR KEBABS.

1/4 cup olive oil
1/3 cup finely chopped garlic
1/3 cup finely chopped shallots
1 large onion, coarsely chopped
2 red bell peppers, coarsely chopped
1 green bell pepper, coarsely chopped
3/4 teaspoon ground black pepper, plus more to taste
3/4 teaspoon salt, plus more to taste
2 pounds firm eggplants (about 2 large; unpeeled),
  cut crosswise into 2-inch slices, each slice quartered
3/4 cup tomato paste
1 1/2 cups water
1 (15 1/2-ounce) can garbanzo beans,
  drained and rinsed

Heat the oil in a deep large nonstick frying pan over medium heat. Add the garlic and shallots, and sauté until fragrant and tender, about 1 minute. Add the onion and bell peppers, and sauté until the onions are translucent and peppers are tender, about 10 minutes. Stir in 3/4 teaspoon of each black pepper and salt. Add the eggplant pieces and cook until they begin to soften, stirring often, about 5 minutes. Stir in the tomato paste, then the water and beans. Bring the cooking liquid to a boil over high heat. Cover and simmer over low heat until the eggplant is tender, stirring occasionally, about 50 minutes. Uncover and continue cooking until the sauce thickens and the eggplant is very tender and soft, stirring occasionally, about 25 minutes. Season the eggplant tagine with more black pepper and salt to taste.

Spoon the eggplant tagine into a large bowl and serve.

COOK'S NOTES: Remember, if eggplant is not cooked until it's tender, it will have a slightly bitter taste. For this dish, the eggplant should become so tender it's mushy.

When shopping, look for firm eggplants with healthy green stem ends, as this indicates freshness.

The eggplant tagine will keep for 2 days, covered and refrigerated. To reheat, add 1/4 cup of water to the mixture, then cover and bring it to a simmer over medium heat, stirring occasionally.

Serves 6 to 8

ROASTED POTATOES WITH PARSLEY AND THYME

YUKON GOLD POTATOES REALLY MAKE THIS DISH. THEIR TEXTURE IS DELIGHTFULLY CREAMIER THAN OTHER POTATOES, AND THEIR FLAVOR HAS A SUBTLE SWEETNESS. SERVE THESE POTATOES AS A SIDE TO THE MARINATED FLANK STEAK (PAGE 156) OR HERB ROASTED CHICKEN (PAGE 169). THEY MAKE DELICIOUS BREAKFAST POTATOES, TOO, ESPECIALLY SINCE THE PREPARATIONS CAN BE DONE THE NIGHT BEFORE.

1 tablespoon plus 1/3 cup olive oil
4 pounds small Yukon gold potatoes
  (about 2-inch-diameter), unpeeled, quartered
1 tablespoon coarsely chopped fresh Italian parsley
1 tablespoon coarsely chopped fresh thyme
1 tablespoon minced shallot
2 teaspoons kosher or sea salt
1/2 teaspoon ground black pepper

Preheat the oven to 375°F. Brush 1 tablespoon of oil over a heavy large rimmed baking sheet. Bring a large pot of water to a boil over high heat. Add the potatoes. Cover and return the water to a boil. Drain. The potatoes should still be firm at this point, but will become tender as they roast in the oven.

Whisk the remaining 1/3 cup of oil, parsley, thyme, shallot, salt, and pepper in a large bowl to blend. Add the potatoes and toss to coat. Arrange the potatoes cut side down on the prepared baking sheet. Roast until the potatoes are almost tender, about 25 minutes. Turn the potatoes skin side down and bake until they are golden brown and tender inside, about 10 minutes longer.

COOK'S NOTES: You can boil the potatoes and toss them with the oil, parsley, thyme, shallots, salt and pepper 1 day ahead. Keep them covered and refrigerated, then just roast them before serving.

Serves 6 to 8

PENNE ARRABBIATA

ARRABBIATA MEANS "ANGRY" IN ITALIAN AND REFERS TO THE SPICINESS OF THE SAUCE THAT COATS THE PASTA. HERE, A CREAMY RICH TOMATO HERB SAUCE, WHICH IS NOT SPICY-HOT AT ALL, IT IS USED AS THE BASE FOR THE ARRABBIATA SAUCE AND BALANCES THE FIERY FLAVORS FROM THE CRUSHED RED PEPPERS THAT ARE ADDED.

1/4 cup olive oil
1/4 cup thinly sliced fresh basil
3 tablespoons minced garlic
2 tablespoons minced shallots
1 teaspoon dried crushed red pepper
1 teaspoon ground black pepper
1 teaspoon salt
5 cups Basic Tomato Herb Sauce (recipe follows)
1 pound dried penne
1/3 cup freshly grated Parmesan cheese,
  plus more for passing
2 tablespoons chopped fresh Italian parsley

Heat the oil in a deep large nonstick frying pan over medium heat. Add the basil, garlic, and shallots, and sauté until the shallots are tender, 1 minute. Add the crushed red pepper, black pepper, and salt. Cook until fragrant, about 1 minute. Stir in the Basic Tomato Herb Sauce. Simmer over low heat for the flavors to blend, about 2 minutes.

Meanwhile, cook the penne in a large pot of boiling salted water until tender but still firm to the bite, stirring occasionally, about 8 minutes. Drain the penne (do not rinse), then add it to the sauce in the pan. Toss to coat over medium heat. Transfer the pasta to a large serving bowl. Sprinkle 1/3 cup of Parmesan cheese and chopped parsley. Serve, passing additional Parmesan cheese separately.

COOK'S NOTES: It is important not to rinse the pasta after it's cooked, as this washes away the starch that helps the sauce cling to the pasta. If you'd like to cook the penne ahead of time, toss it with a bit of olive oil after draining it to keep the penne from sticking together. When you're ready to serve, submerge the penne in a large pot of boiling salted water just until it's heated through, then drain it and toss it with the sauce.

Any type of pasta will work in this dish. Linguine, fusilli, or spaghetti are some of my favorites. For variation, serve it with chicken, salmon, or shrimp.

Serves 6

BASIC TOMATO HERB SAUCE

THIS IS MY PREFERRED DELICIOUS MARINARA SAUCE, I LIKE TO USE FOR PASTAS, CASSEROLES, OR THE BASE FOR TOMATO SOUPS.

1/4 cup olive oil
1/2 cup (lightly packed) coarsely
  chopped fresh basil
1/2 cup (lightly packed) coarsely
  chopped fresh Italian parsley
1/4 cup chopped garlic
1/4 cup chopped shallots
2 (28-ounce) cans whole tomatoes with juice
2 teaspoons salt
1 teaspoon ground black pepper
3 tablespoons unsalted butter

Heat the oil in a heavy medium saucepan over medium-high heat. Add the basil, parsley, garlic, and shallots and sauté until fragrant, about 1 minute. Add the tomatoes, salt, and pepper. Bring the sauce to a simmer. Decrease the heat to low. Cover and simmer the sauce until the tomatoes are tender, stirring occasionally, about 20 minutes, and breaking up the tomatoes with the back of the spoon. Uncover to cool the sauce slightly. Working in batches, blend the tomato mixture and butter in a blender until smooth.

COOK'S NOTES: This recipe makes a generous amount of sauce for one pound of pasta.

I like to keep this sauce handy for quick last minute meals. It keeps well for up to 1 week in the refrigerator, and 1 month in the freezer.

You can be creative by adding the sauce to your favorite stews.

Makes about 6 cups

EGGPLANT STUFFED WITH GARLIC

THERE'S NO BETTER WAY TO INDULGE IN SUMMER'S BOUNTY THAN WITH THIS TASTY SIDE DISH. THESE EGGPLANTS ARE GREAT WITH STEAKS, KEBABS, OR SEAFOOD, AND DELICIOUS WITH PASTA, RICE, OR COUSCOUS. THEY ALSO MAKE A PERFECT FIRST COURSE OR VEGETARIAN ENTRÉE. AND, BECAUSE THEY CAN BE SERVED WARM OR COLD, THEY MAKE A GREAT PICNIC DISH.

8 Japanese eggplants (about 3 ounces each)
3 tablespoons olive oil plus 1/4 cup
24 small garlic cloves, peeled, or
*   12 large garlic cloves, halved*
2 medium onions, thinly sliced
1 large green bell pepper, diced
1 large red bell pepper, diced
5 plum tomatoes, seeded and diced
5 tablespoons tomato paste
3 tablespoons minced garlic
1 cup warm water
3 tablespoons chopped fresh parsley
1 1/4 teaspoons ground black pepper
1 1/4 teaspoons salt

Preheat the oven to 350°F. Line a plate with paper towels. Cut three 1-inch-long slits down one side of each eggplant. Stuff the slits with the garlic cloves. Heat 3 tablespoons of oil in a deep large nonstick frying pan over medium-high heat. Place the eggplants, stuffed side down, in the skillet and cook until they darken on the bottom, about 3 minutes. Turn the eggplants over and cook until they darken on the bottom, about 3 minutes longer. Transfer the eggplants to the prepared plate to soak up any excess oil.

Heat the remaining 1/4 cup of oil in the same skillet over high heat. Add the onions and bell peppers, and sauté until the onions are translucent and soft, about 5 minutes. Mix in the tomatoes, tomato paste, and minced garlic. Stir in the water. Simmer until the mixture thickens and the tomatoes are tender, stirring often, about 10 minutes (the sauce will be chunky). Stir in 2 tablespoons of parsley, and the black pepper and salt.

Spoon half of the tomato sauce over the bottom of a 13x9x2-inch glass-baking dish. Arrange the eggplants side by side atop the sauce, then spoon the remaining tomato sauce over and around the eggplants. Cover with foil and bake until the eggplants are very soft and mushy, about 50 minutes. Uncover and continue baking until the liquid evaporates, about 15 minutes longer. Sprinkle with the remaining 1 tablespoon of parsley and serve immediately. Alternately, transfer the eggplants and tomato sauce to a platter then set aside until cool, and serve at room temperature.

COOK'S NOTES: Be certain to select firm eggplants that are about 4 to 6 inches in length and about 2 inches wide.

The eggplants and tomato sauce keep for up to 3 days, covered and refrigerated. They're delicious cold or room temperature, but to rewarm them simply cover the baking dish with foil and bake at 350°F until the eggplants are heated through, about 30 minutes.

Serves 8

MEAT

AND POULTRY

Surprisingly easy recipes help the cook grill, sauté, braise, and stew by seasoning with lively aromatics, such as mint, cilantro, dill, flat parsley, coriander, cumin, saffron, and cinnamon. The herbs and spices add rich color and flavor to delicious meats, such as the Roasted Rack of Lamb with Pomegranate Sauce—so succulent the flavor bursts in your mouth!

SAN FRANCISCO 1960

On chilly winter afternoons in San Francisco, when the thick fog never seemed to fully lift from the city, I would return home from school to a house full of the warmth of cooking. Our kitchen was tiny, but my brothers, sisters and I, and often our friends, would constantly migrate to the well-lit room, especially when mother baked her 'little pizzas'. I remember the way she used her whole arm to fold the fragrant mixture of puréed red and green peppers, parsley and onions into the large bowl of finely-ground beef. She'd mince the garlic separately, its rich aroma fusing with the slight fruitiness of the peppers. The flatbread dough she'd make next, mixing and kneading and pulling until it was quite thick and springy. Her gold bracelets jingled as she flicked oil onto the dough to keep it dry, then worked sections into small round balls from where she would spread them flat with her strong, straight fingers. The dough became disks as she worked them around, pressing the meat mixture down into the crust. Heaven must smell as good as our kitchen did when those pizzas were cooking: the meat's spiciness and the bread's slight sweetness drew everyone in. As soon as mother brought them out of the oven, we'd eat them, warm, the crust slightly golden, crunchy, but soft enough to fold. She'd scold us lightly for eating too many, but we just couldn't stop.

I chose to include this recipe as an appetizer on our menu in part to honor my mother and all those warm, wonderful afternoons. It's the texture of this pizza and the slight spicy-sweetness of it that makes it irresistible. But you can build on this recipe as we do at the bistro. For instance, we sprinkle grated Parmigiano-Reggiano cheese over the crust, then crumble a bit of feta cheese over the meat, and add diced, fresh plum tomatoes. The cheese melts slightly. Delicious! We slice it into wedges, but you could roll it up and serve it as a wrap. Try adding grilled eggplant or zucchini slices. The little pizzas make a great snacks. Freeze them (baked and cooled), and warm them later for an afternoon treat.

FLATBREADS WITH SPICED GROUND BEEF (LAHMAJOUNE)

BE SURE TO MAKE ENOUGH OF THESE LITTLE BEEF PIZZAS SO THAT YOUR FAMILY CAN ENJOY THEM FRESH FROM THE OVEN. THEY WON'T BE ABLE TO RESIST SAMPLING THEM! CONVENIENTLY, THESE FLATBREADS FREEZE VERY WELL (SEE COOK'S NOTES BELOW).

Spiced Beef Topping

3 garlic cloves
3/4 cup coarsely chopped onion
1/2 cup coarsely chopped red bell pepper
1/4 cup coarsely chopped green bell pepper
1/4 cup chopped fresh Italian parsley
1 cup canned whole tomatoes
8 ounces lean ground beef
1/4 cup tomato paste
1 teaspoon crushed dried mint
1 teaspoon ground black pepper
1 teaspoon lemon pepper
1 teaspoon salt
1 teaspoon seasoned salt

Dough

1 cup warm water (105°F to 115°F)
2 (1/4-ounce) envelopes dry yeast
1 teaspoon sugar
1/2 cup about olive oil
1 teaspoon salt
4 1/2 cups all purpose flour

For the spiced beef topping: Mince the garlic cloves in the food processor. Add the onion, red and green peppers, and parsley. Pulse just until the vegetables are finely diced (do not puree). Add the tomatoes to the vegetables, and pulse just until the mixture is blended. Transfer the vegetable-tomato mixture to a large bowl. Add the beef, tomato paste, mint, black pepper, lemon pepper, salt, and seasoned salt. Knead the ingredients with your hands until the mixture is well blended. Cover and refrigerate until ready to use. (The beef meat mixture can be prepared 1 day ahead. Keep refrigerated.)

For the dough: Mix the warm water, yeast, and sugar in the food processor. Let stand until the yeast dissolves and the mixture is foamy, about 10 minutes. Blend in 2 tablespoons of oil. Add the salt then 4 cups of flour.

Blend just until a thick dough forms. Dust the work surface with the remaining 1/2 cup of flour. Transfer the dough to the work surface and knead until the dough is smooth and elastic, about 1 minute.

Lightly oil a large bowl. Transfer the dough to the bowl, turning the dough to coat it with the oil. Cover with plastic and a kitchen towel. Set it aside in a warm, draft-free area until the dough doubles in volume, about 1 1/2 hours.

To assemble the flatbreads: Position the rack on the bottom of the oven and preheat the oven to 450°F. Line a heavy large baking sheet with plastic. Punch the dough down. Transfer the dough to a work surface. Using a large sharp knife, cut the dough into 12 equal pieces. Shape each dough piece into a ball, placing them on the prepared baking sheet as you go. Cover with plastic and let the dough balls rest for 10 minutes (this will allow the dough to relax, making it easier to roll out).

Lightly oil 2 heavy large baking sheets. Roll out each of 4 dough balls on a lightly floured work surface into 5- to 6-inch-diameter circles. Arrange the 4 dough circles on one prepared baking sheet. Spread 3 tablespoons of the beef mixture over the entire surface of each dough circle. Bake until the tops and bottoms of the flatbreads are crisp and golden, about 16 minutes. Working in two more batches, repeat with the remaining 8 dough balls and beef mixture.

COOK'S NOTES: Lahmajoune may be baked and then kept frozen for up to 3 months. To freeze, place a 4 by 4-inch piece of wax paper between each flatbread before freezing to help separate them when removing them from the freezer. To reheat the frozen flatbreads, place them on a baking sheet, and bake at 450°F for 5 minutes or until they are warm and crisp.

Chopped fresh tomatoes or halved cherry tomatoes tossed with chopped fresh rosemary, salt, and pepper make a delicious topping for these savory flatbreads. Shredded Parmesan cheese and grilled eggplant slices make terrific toppings too. Form the flatbreads into smaller rounds to serve them as cocktail appetizers.

Some delis offer already-made pizza dough, which will work quite well for these pies. You can substitute refrigerated biscuit dough for the crust, too. But course, nothing beats a homemade crust for this recipe!

Makes 12 flatbreads

ROAST PORK RACK WITH SOUR CHERRY SAUCE

THIS SUCCULENT, TENDER ROAST IS EASY TO PREPARE. THE SHARP FLAVOR OF SOUR CHERRIES BALANCES THE EARTHINESS OF MOROCCAN SPICES. SERVE THE PORK ROAST WITH SAUTÉED ASPARAGUS AND CARROTS, AND MASHED POTATOES, ROASTED POTATOES, OR A POTATO GRATIN.

Pork Roast

1 (4- to 5-pound) pork rib roast
  with 7 or 8 ribs (see Cook's Notes)
1 tablespoon ground black pepper
1 tablespoon salt
2 tablespoons Moroccan Spices (page 200)

Sour Cherry Sauce

2 tablespoons olive oil
3 tablespoons minced garlic
3 tablespoons minced shallots
1 1/2 cups Marsala wine
1 pound fresh or frozen pitted tart cherries,
  thawed if frozen
1 3/4 cups beef stock or broth (from one 14-ounce can)
4 tablespoons (1/2 stick) chilled unsalted butter,
  cut into 1/2-inch pieces
  Salt and ground black pepper, to taste

To make the pork roast: Preheat the oven to 425°F. Place the pork bone-side down in the center of a large shallow roasting pan. Rub the pepper and salt all over the pork, then generously rub the Moroccan Spices all over the pork. Roast until an instant-read meat thermometer registers 135°F when inserted into the center of the meat, about 1 hour. Remove the pork from the oven and let it cool for about 10 minutes (as the pork cools, the temperature will increase to 150°F).

Meanwhile, prepare the sour cherry sauce: Heat the oil in a heavy large saucepan over medium heat. Add the garlic and shallots, and sauté until tender, about 2 minutes. Stir in the Marsala. Increase the heat to medium-high and simmer for 2 minutes. Stir in three-fourths of the cherries and all of the broth. Bring the mixture to a boil. Reduce the heat to medium and simmer uncovered until the cooking liquid reduces by half and thickens slightly, stirring occasionally, about 35 minutes. Stir in the remaining cherries. Remove from the heat. Stir in the butter one piece at a time until well blended. Season the sauce to taste with salt and pepper.

Cut the pork between the rib bones into 4 slices (with 2 ribs per slice), or cut the pork into 8 slices (with 1 rib per slice). Place the pork on plates. Spoon the sauce over the pork and serve.

COOK'S NOTES: Classic rib rack is served with the rib bones exposed, or "frenched." Ask the butcher to trim your pork rack for you, if desired, as it will save you a lot of time. You can use boneless pork roast, but the bones make the meat much more tender and succulent.

Prunes or dates can be substituted for the cherries in the sauce.

Serves 4

ROASTED RACK OF LAMB WITH POMEGRANATE SAUCE

MORE AND MORE PEOPLE ARE DISCOVERING THE TENDER, SUCCULENT QUALITIES OF LAMB. WHEN COOKED RIGHT, IT'S ABSOLUTELY UNFORGETTABLE. THE TRICK IS TO SEAR ALL THE SIDES IN A VERY HOT PAN, WITHOUT MOVING THE LAMB. THE POMEGRANATE MOLASSES ADDS A SAVORY SWEETNESS TO THE SAUCE THAT YOUR GUESTS WILL FIND WONDERFULLY UNIQUE. TENDER AND DELICIOUS, THIS LAMB IS JUST RIGHT WHEN SERVED ON A BED OF MASHED POTATOES OR WITH CLASSIC RICE PILAF (PAGE 133). I ALSO SUGGEST SERVING THE EGGPLANT TAGINE (PAGE 139) AS A SIDE DISH.

Lamb
1/4 cup plus 1 tablespoon olive oil
1 tablespoon coarsely ground black pepper
1 tablespoon chopped fresh rosemary
1 tablespoon chopped fresh thyme
1 tablespoon minced garlic
1 tablespoon salt
2 (1 1/2 pounds each) racks of lamb
    trimmed, (see Cook's Notes)
3 tablespoons Dijon mustard

Pomegranate Sauce
1 tablespoon olive oil
2 tablespoons minced shallot
1 tablespoon minced garlic
1 cup reduced-sodium beef broth or stock
1/4 cup pomegranate molasses (page 13)
4 tablespoons (1/2 stick) chilled unsalted butter,
    cut into 4 pieces
    Salt and ground black pepper, to taste
    Pomegranate seeds, for garnish

Stir 1/4 cup oil, black pepper, rosemary, thyme, garlic, and salt in a small bowl to blend. Rub all but 2 tablespoons of the oil mixture over both sides of the lamb racks. Mix the mustard into the remaining oil mixture in the bowl. Cover the lamb and mustard mixture separately. Refrigerate at least 2 hours or up to 1 day.

Preheat the oven to 400°F. Heat the remaining 1 tablespoon of oil in a heavy large oven proof skillet (make sure the skillet is large enough to fit both lamb racks) over medium-high heat until it is almost smoking (you should see a slight smoke rising from the skillet). Place the lamb racks in the skillet and cook just until brown, about 4 minutes per side. Arrange the lamb racks rounded side up in the skillet. Spread the mustard mixture over each. Roast the lamb in the oven until cooked to desired doneness, about 20 minutes for medium-rare. Transfer the lamb racks to a work surface (do not clean the skillet). Tent loosely with foil to keep warm.

Meanwhile, prepare the pomegranate sauce: Drain the accumulated fat from the skillet that the lamb was roasted in. Heat the oil in the skillet over medium-high heat. Add the shallot and garlic, and sauté until fragrant and tender, about 1 minute. Whisk in the broth and pomegranate molasses. Increase the heat to high, and boil the sauce until it reduces by half and is syrupy, about 8 minutes. Remove the skillet from the heat. Whisk the butter into the sauce 1 piece at a time until well blended. Season the sauce to taste with salt and pepper.

Cut the lamb between the bones. Arrange the lamb chops on plates, overlapping slightly. Spoon the sauce generously over and around each serving. Garnish with the pomegranate seeds and serve immediately.

COOK'S NOTES: When purchasing rack of lamb, be sure the meat is well trimmed of fat. To eliminate last minute preparations, sear the lamb then coat it with the mustard mixture up to 1 day before serving it. Then cover the lamb and refrigerate. When you're just about ready to serve dinner, roast the lamb as directed above, and make the sauce.

Serves 4 to 6

MARINATED FLANK STEAKS WITH GINGER, SOY, AND GARLIC

THERE ARE SO MANY WAYS TO COOK FLANK STEAK, BUT I PREFER TO GRILL IT, ADDING ANOTHER DIMENSION OF FLAVORS TO THE MEAT. THE GINGER AND SOY IN THE MARINADE LEND GREAT ASIATIC FLAVORS TO THE STEAKS. SERVE THEM WITH THE EGGPLANT AND AVOCADO SALSA (PAGE 29) OR ROASTED POTATOES WITH PARSLEY AND THYME (PAGE 140).

1 bunch green onions, coarsely chopped
1/2 cup soy sauce
1/2 cup (lightly packed) fresh cilantro leaves
1/4 cup (lightly packed) fresh mint leaves
1/4 cup toasted sesame oil
3 tablespoons fresh lemon juice
1 jalapeño chile, coarsely chopped
1 (1-inch) piece fresh ginger, peeled and
*   finely chopped*
5 garlic cloves
2 (1 1/2-pound) flank steaks,
*   trimmed of fat and sinew*

Blend the first 9 ingredients in a food processor until the green onions are very finely chopped and the mixture is almost smooth. Pour the marinade into a 13x9x2-inch baking dish. Add the flank steaks and turn to coat with the marinade. Cover and refrigerate at least 2 hours or up to 1 day, turning the steaks occasionally.

Prepare the barbecue for medium-high heat. Pour the marinade into a small saucepan and bring it to a boil over medium-high heat. Set the sauce aside.

Grill the steaks until brown on the bottom, about 5 minutes. Turn the steaks over. Generously brush the sauce over the steaks. Continue grilling to desired doneness, about 5 minutes longer for medium-rare (avoid over-cooking the steaks since cooking flank steak to well-done will destroy the flavor and texture). Transfer the steaks to a work surface and let them stand for 10 minutes.

Cut the steaks across the grain into thin strips. Arrange on a platter and serve. Pass any remaining sauce separately.

COOK'S NOTES: The purpose of marinating flank steak is to tenderize the meat, a process that requires an acid in the marinade. The acidity of the marinade, from lemon juice in this case, causes the protein in the muscles of the meat to break down. The result is a wonderful piece of meat that is truly tender and delicious.

To broil the steaks, position the oven rack 6 inches below the broiler and preheat the broiler. Arrange the steaks on a broiler pan and broil until brown on top, about 5 minutes. Turn the steaks over and brush the sauce over the top. Continue broiling until the steaks are brown and cooked to medium-rare, about 5 minutes longer.

Be sure to bring the marinade to a boil before using it as a sauce.

Consider topping the steaks with caramelized onions. To caramelize onions, slice them thinly, then place them in a heavy skillet over high heat with a few tablespoons of olive oil and sauté until they are dark brown.

Serves 6 to 8

SPINACH-STUFFED
LEG OF LAMB

WHEN LAMB IS SERVED, YOU KNOW IT'S SPRING.
AND THIS EASY, FLAVORFUL DISH, MAKES SUCH
A WONDERFUL ITEM FOR A HOLIDAY BUFFET
TABLE. SERVE THE SLICES OF LAMB ON A BED
OF BRAISED SPINACH AND SURROUND THE
PLATES WITH ROASTED POTATOES AND
CARROTS. SPOON MUSHROOM, TOMATO AND
WHITE WINE SAUCE (PAGE 192) OVER THIS
DELICIOUS DISH. ANY LEFTOVER LAMB MAKE
TERRIFIC AND SATISFYING SANDWICHES, TOO.

1 (4- to 5-pound) boneless leg of lamb,
  butterflied, fat and sinew trimmed
5 tablespoons olive oil
3 tablespoons Dijon mustard
2 1/2 teaspoons coarsely cracked black pepper
1 1/2 teaspoons salt
3 tablespoons chopped fresh Italian parsley
3 tablespoons chopped fresh rosemary
3 tablespoons finely chopped garlic
2 tablespoons chopped fresh thyme
5 ounces fresh spinach, thinly sliced
1/4 cup pine nuts, toasted (page 18)

Pat the lamb dry with paper towels. Lay the butterflied
lamb cut side up on the work surface. Using a meat
mallet, pound the lamb until it is evenly about 1-inch
thick. Rub 3 tablespoons of the oil and mustard over
both sides of the lamb. Then, massage the pepper
and salt into the meat (the marinade will help break
down the fibers and allows the meat to absorb the
seasonings). Spread the, parsley, rosemary, garlic and
thyme over both sides of the lamb. Mound the spinach
and pine nuts evenly down the center of the meat.
Starting at one short end of the lamb, roll up the lamb
tightly, as a jellyroll. Since the meat is not shaped like a
perfect rectangle, pieces may stick out from the sides.
Just tuck them in as you go and keep rolling.
Tie the roast with kitchen twine, first securing it around
the middle with short individual strings, and spacing
the strings about 1 inch apart. Finish tying the roast
securely with a long string that will wrap around the
roast twice lengthwise and loop around each of the short
individual strings. Cover and refrigerate overnight.

Preheat the oven to 400°F. Heat the remaining
2 tablespoons of oil in a heavy large skillet over
medium-high heat. Cook the lamb just until it is
brown on all sides, about 8 minutes. Transfer the
lamb to a large shallow roasting pan and roast until
an instant-read meat thermometer registers 120°F
for rare to medium-rare, about 1 hour. Remove the
lamb from the oven and let rest for 10 minutes before
carving (the temperature will rise to 130°F as it rests).

Remove all the strings from the lamb. Using a large
sharp knife cut the lamb crosswise into 1/2-inch-
thick slices. Arrange the sliced lamb on a platter and
serve immediately.

COOK'S NOTES: Stuffing the lamb a day before allows the
flavors to penetrate the meat. Use thick cotton string so
that it won't burn in the oven or cut into the meat. If you
do not like your meat rare or medium-rare, roast it until
the instant-read meat thermometer registers 145°F to
150°F for medium, and 160°F for well-done.

Slice only the amount of lamb that you need and leave
the remaining roast whole so that it stays warm and
does not dry out.

Serves 6 to 8

SAVORY MINCED BEEF KEBABS WITH ONION-SUMAC RELISH

THESE KEBABS ARE REMINISCENT OF THE STREET FOOD IN THE MIDDLE EAST, INDIA, MOROCCO, AND SOUTHEAST ASIA. THEIR INTOXICATING AROMA WILL DELIGHT YOUR FAMILY AND GUESTS. FRESH CILANTRO AND MINT ENHANCES THE FLAVORS OF THE MEAT. TRY THE KEBABS GRILLED AND SERVED AS A SANDWICH IN PITA BREAD OR SOFT LAVASH. TOP THEM WITH CUCUMBERS, CILANTRO, MINT, TOMATOES, THINLY SLICED CABBAGE, AND THE ONION-SUMAC RELISH. DELICIOUS!

Kebabs

1 1/2 pounds lean ground beef
1 small onion, finely minced (about 3/4 cup)
1/4 cup finely chopped fresh cilantro
1/4 cup finely chopped fresh Italian parsley
1/4 cup finely chopped fresh mint
1 jalapeño chile, minced
2 teaspoons salt
1 teaspoon ground black pepper
1/8 teaspoon ground allspice
1/8 teaspoon ground cinnamon

Onion-sumac Relish

1 small red onion, very thinly sliced
3 tablespoons ground sumac (page 13)
1/2 cup chopped fresh Italian parsley
1/2 cup chopped fresh mint

To make the kebabs: Using your hands, mix all the ingredients in a large bowl until well blended. Divide the meat mixture into 8 equal mounds. Shape each mound of meat mixture into a sausage-shaped patty. Insert a metal skewer at one end and push it through to the opposite end of each patty.

To make the relish: Toss the onion with the sumac in a medium bowl to coat. Squeeze the onion mixture to extract as much juice as possible from the onion. Discard the juice. Stir the parsley and mint into the onion mixture

Prepare the barbecue for high heat. Grill the kebabs until just cooked through, turning occasionally, about 10 minutes. Transfer the kebabs to a platter and serve immediately with the relish.

COOK'S NOTES: An alternative is to shape the beef into patties and serve it with Tzatziki sauce (page 182), or Tahini Sauce (page 34). If you prefer to use it as a main entrée, line a platter with mint leaves and slices of tomatoes, feta cheese, fresh cilantro, chives, and side bowl of Tahini Sauce or Tzatziki sauce.

The kebabs can be prepared up to 1 day ahead before grilling. And the relish can be prepared 8 hours ahead. Cover the kebabs and relish separately and refrigerate.

Serves 4 to 8

GRILLED SKEWERED LAMB AND VEGETABLES

THIS RECIPE IS THE MIDDLE EASTERN VERSION OF KEBABS. IT'S TRADITIONALLY MADE WITH DELICIOUS LAMB THAT'S MOST SUCCULENT WHEN COOKED MEDIUM-RARE. SERVE THE KEBABS ON A BED OF CLASSIC RICE PILAF (PAGE 133), WITH THE EGGPLANT TAGINE (PAGE 139), OR WITH THE ONION-SUMAC RELISH (PAGE 160).

Lamb Kebabs
12 lamb loin chops (about 4 1/2 pounds)
2 large onions, thinly sliced
2 lemons, thinly sliced
1/4 cup olive oil
2 tablespoons coarsely ground black pepper (page 18)
2 tablespoons soy sauce
1 tablespoon salt

Vegetable Kebabs
1/4 cup olive oil
1 1/2 tablespoons finely chopped fresh rosemary
1 teaspoon ground black pepper
1 teaspoon salt
12 large white mushrooms
4 small red bell peppers,
  each cut into 6 large chunks
2 large Japanese eggplants,
each cut crosswise into 6 pieces
2 large zucchini,
  each cut crosswise into 6 pieces

To make the lamb kebabs: Using a sharp knife, remove the two pieces of meat from each chop. Trim away any fat and sinew from the meat. Cut the larger pieces of meat crosswise in half. Toss the onions, lemon slices, oil, pepper, soy sauce, and salt in a large bowl. Add the meat. Using your hands, massage the marinade into the meat. Cover and refrigerate for at least 4 hours or up to 2 days, stirring occasionally. Thread 6 pieces of the lamb onto each of 6 skewers, spacing the meat 1/2-inch apart. Cover and refrigerate until ready to grill.

To make the vegetable kebabs: Whisk the oil, rosemary, black pepper, and salt, in a large bowl to blend. Add the vegetables and toss to coat. Let stand up to 1 hour at room temperature, tossing occasionally. Thread 1 mushroom, 4 pieces of bell pepper, 2 pieces of eggplant, and 2 pieces of zucchini alternately onto each of 6 skewers.

Prepare the barbecue for high heat. Grill the lamb until it is crisp and brown on the outside but pink in the center, turning occasionally, about 8 minutes. Grill the vegetable kebabs until the vegetables are tender and beginning to char, turning occasionally, about 8 minutes.

Arrange the skewers on plates and serve.

COOK'S NOTES: Lamb loin chops make especially delicious kebabs because they are the most tender cut of lamb. And, once trimmed, the lamb loin is free of gristle and fat. Ask your butcher to bone the lamb loin chops for you, making this a cinch to put together. If lamb loin is not available, boneless leg of lamb is a good substitute, just but be sure to remove as much gristle and fat as possible. And, if desired, beef tenderloin can be used instead of the lamb loin.

Serve the skewers on a platter accompanied with feta cheese, cilantro, fresh mint, olives, cucumber slices, tomatoes, walnuts, and a bowl of Tzatziki Sauce (page 182), Onion-sumac Relish (page 160), and warm pita bread wedges.

Serves 6

GRILLED CHICKEN WITH FRESH HERBS AND TOMATO COMPOTE

THIS IS A VERY SIMPLE RECIPE, YET THE DISH HAS SUCH BOLD FLAVORS. CINNAMON IS THE SECRET INGREDIENT THAT LENDS A UNIQUE TASTE. SERVE THE CLASSIC RICE PILAF (PAGE 133), ROASTED POTATOES WITH PARSLEY AND THYME (PAGE 140), OR BUTTERED PASTA ALONGSIDE.

Chicken

1/4 cup fresh lemon juice
3 tablespoons olive oil
2 tablespoons finely chopped fresh Italian parsley
2 tablespoons finely chopped fresh oregano
1 teaspoon salt
1/2 teaspoon ground black pepper
1/2 teaspoon lemon pepper
1/2 teaspoon sweet paprika
1/8 teaspoon ground cinnamon
6 boneless skinless chicken breasts
  Nonstick cooking spray

Tomato Compote

2 tablespoons olive oil
12 ounces tomatoes, cut into 1/2-inch pieces
1/4 cup finely chopped red onion
3 tablespoons finely chopped fresh Italian parsley
3 tablespoons finely chopped fresh oregano
2 teaspoons minced garlic
1/2 teaspoon ground black pepper
1/2 teaspoon salt
1/2 cup pine nuts, toasted (page 18)

To cook the chicken: Whisk the lemon juice, oil, parsley, oregano, salt, black pepper, lemon pepper, paprika, and cinnamon in a 13x9x2-inch baking dish. Add the chicken and turn to coat. Cover and refrigerate at least 2 hours and up to 1 day, turning occasionally.

Spray the grill rack with nonstick cooking spray. Prepare the barbecue for medium-high heat. Grill the chicken breasts until they are just cooked through, about 4 minutes per side. The chicken should still be firm to the touch; if it's too firm; it is overcooked and will be dry. So watch it carefully.

Meanwhile, prepare the tomato compote: Heat the oil in a heavy large skillet over medium-high heat. Add the tomatoes, onion, parsley, oregano, garlic, pepper and salt. Sauté just until the tomatoes are heated through, about 2 minutes. Stir in the pine nuts.

Transfer the chicken to a platter. Spoon the warm tomato compote over the chicken and serve.

COOK'S NOTES: Make sure you use fresh herbs, as their oils will infuse the chicken with flavorful nuances. If desired, you can substitute fresh thyme or rosemary for the oregano.

The tomato compote compliments grilled salmon or halibut as well.

Serves 6

COCONUT BEEF STEW WITH CILANTRO AND MINT

UNSWEETENED COCONUT MILK ADDS RICHNESS AND A DISTINCT FLAVOR TO THIS HEARTY BEEF STEW. FLUFFY WHITE RICE, COUSCOUS, OR BUTTERED PASTA MAKE GREAT ACCOMPANIMENTS. ADD A GLASS OF RED WINE AND YOU'VE GOT A FABULOUS MEAL.

3 pounds boneless beef chuck,
  cut into 1- to 1 1/2-inch cubes
3 teaspoons salt
1 teaspoon ground black pepper
2 tablespoons vegetable oil
1 onion, chopped
8 green onions, chopped
2 tablespoons finely chopped peeled fresh ginger
6 ounces white mushrooms, sliced
3 carrots, peeled and
  cut diagonally into 1/4-inch-thick slices
2 tablespoons tomato paste
2 tablespoons minced garlic
1 3/4 cups beef broth
1 cup unsweetened coconut milk
1/2 cup coarsely chopped fresh cilantro
1/2 cup coarsely chopped fresh mint
  Cilantro sprigs, for garnish
  Lemon zest, for garnish

Pat the beef dry with paper towels then sprinkle with 1 teaspoon each of salt and pepper. Heat the oil in a large heavy pot over high heat. Working in two batches, add the beef to the pot and cook just until brown, about 5 minutes. Using a slotted spoon, transfer the beef to a bowl. Add the onion, green onions, and ginger to the same pot. Stir to scrape up the browned bits on the bottom of the pot, about 1 minute. Add the mushrooms and carrots. Sauté until the onions are tender, about 5 minutes. Stir in the tomato paste and garlic. Stir in the broth, coconut milk, chopped cilantro, mint, and remaining 2 teaspoons of salt. Return the beef and any accumulated juices to the pot. Bring the mixture to a simmer. Decrease the heat to low. Cover and cook until the beef is almost tender, stirring occasionally, about 1 hour. Uncover and simmer over medium heat until the liquid reduces by about half and the beef is very tender, stirring occasionally, about 30 minutes longer.

Spoon the stew into bowls. Garnish with the cilantro sprigs and lemon zest, and serve.

COOK'S NOTES: Prepare the stew a day ahead if you'd like, because it tastes even better the next day.

Lemon Zest is the outer layer of the lemon.

Coconut milk is available in most grocery stores or Indian markets.

Serves 6 to 8

HERB ROASTED CHICKEN

THE SUCCESS OF COOKING A DELICIOUS ROASTED CHICKEN IS IN THE DETAILS. THE TEMPERATURE OF THE OVEN MUST BE HIGH TO START WITH, THEN LOWERED A BIT TO SEAL IN THE JUICES. IT IS THE INITIAL HIGH HEAT THAT ALSO ALLOWS THE SKIN TO DEVELOP A DELICIOUS CRISP TEXTURE AND RICH DEEP COLOR. SERVE THE CHICKEN WITH ROASTED POTATOES WITH PARSLEY AND THYME (PAGE 140) AND A GREEK SALAD (PAGE 74).

1 (3 1/2-pound) whole chicken
3 tablespoons unsalted butter
2 tablespoons chopped fresh thyme
1 tablespoon coarsely ground black pepper
2 tablespoons finely chopped garlic
1 tablespoon chopped fresh rosemary
1 tablespoon salt
1 teaspoon paprika
4 large rosemary sprigs
4 large thyme sprigs
1 small red onion, peeled and cut into 8 wedges
2 lemons, 1 quartered, 1 thinly sliced
1 head garlic, halved crosswise
2 bay leaves
1/2 cup water

Position the rack inside the oven so that the chicken will roast in the center of the oven, then preheat the oven to 450°F. Remove the giblets from inside the chicken. Rinse the chicken inside and out, then pat dry. Place the chicken, breast side up, on a v-shaped roasting rack set inside a roasting pan. Pull away the lumps of fat attached to the skin of the chicken just near the opening. You may discard these or add them to the roasting pan to add a bit more richness to the sauce.

Stir the butter, chopped thyme, black pepper, garlic, chopped rosemary, salt, and paprika in a small saucepan over medium-low heat just until the butter melts. Starting at the neck end, carefully slide your hand between the skin and breast meat to loosen the skin. Stuff 2 sprigs of each the rosemary and thyme over the breast meat and under the skin, then drizzle some of the herb butter over the breast meat. Brush some herb butter inside the chicken cavity. Place the onion, quartered lemon, garlic halves, bay leaves, and the remaining 2 sprigs of each rosemary and thyme in the chicken cavity. Tie the legs together loosely with kitchen string to help hold the shape of the chicken. Rub the remaining herb butter over the chicken.

Roast the chicken, uncovered, for 15 minutes. Decrease the heat to 350°F and continue roasting the chicken, basting occasionally with the pan drippings, until the chicken is golden brown and an instant-read meat thermometer inserted into the thickest part of the chicken thigh registers 160°F, about 55 minutes longer. Using a carving fork, tilt the chicken so that the juices from the chicken cavity drain into the pan. Transfer chicken to a platter. Garnish with the lemon slices and roasted garlic. Tent with foil.

Set the roasting pan on the stove and over medium heat. Add 1/2 cup of water to the pan and bring to a simmer, scraping up the browned bits. Pour the pan juices into a large glass measuring cup. Spoon off and discard the fat. Serve the au jus alongside the chicken.

COOK'S NOTES: Using fresh herbs makes a huge difference, as they'll lend vibrancy to the flavors. The chicken should be plump and fresh, and weigh anywhere from 4 1/2 to 5 pounds, but no larger.

Serves 4 to 6

CHICKEN MARSALA WITH FUSILLI PASTA

I LOVE COOKING WITH MARSALA, A DESSERT-LIKE WINE FROM WESTERN SICILY. IT'S BECAUSE OF THE MARSALA THAT THIS DISH BOASTS A SUBTLY SWEET TASTE. OFFER THE PASTA AS A LIGHT DINNER ENTRÉE FOLLOWING THE ROMAINE SALAD WITH HEARTS OF PALM AND ARTICHOKES (PAGE 64). FOR DESSERT, SERVE THE AMBER-COLORED MARSALA WINE (I LIKE IT CHILLED) WITH DRY, SALTY CHEESES SUCH AS PARMESAN OR A CREAMY BLUE-VEINED CHEESE LIKE SPANISH CABRALES, GORGONZOLA, OR ROQUEFORT. THE SWEETNESS OF THE WINE REALLY COMPLEMENTS THE RICHNESS OF THE CHEESES AND FINISHES THIS PASTA DISH BEAUTIFULLY.

2 tablespoons unsalted butter
1 tablespoon olive oil
12 ounces boneless skinless chicken breasts,
    cut into 3/4-inch cubes
1 teaspoon ground black pepper
1 teaspoon salt
12 ounces white mushrooms, sliced
8 ounces carrots, peeled and thinly sliced diagonally
1/2 cup minced shallots
5 tablespoons minced garlic
1 1/2 cups sun-dried tomatoes (about 5 ounces),
    thinly sliced
1 3/4 cups chicken broth
1 1/2 cups whipping cream
1 1/2 cups Marsala wine
1 pound fusilli (spiral-shaped pasta)
    Thyme sprigs, for garnish

Melt the butter and oil in a deep large nonstick frying pan over medium-high heat. Sprinkle the chicken with 1/2 teaspoon of each pepper and salt. Add the chicken pieces and cook until they're pale golden and just cooked through, about 4 minutes. Using a slotted spoon, transfer the chicken to a large bowl. Set aside.

Add the mushrooms, carrots, and half the shallots and half of garlic to the same pan. Sauté until the liquid from the mushrooms evaporates and the carrots are crisp-tender, about 6 minutes. Using a slotted spoon, transfer the vegetables to the bowl of chicken.

Add the sun-dried tomatoes and rest of the shallots and garlic to the same pan. Sauté until fragrant, about 30 seconds. Stir in the broth, cream, Marsala, and remaining 1/2 teaspoon of each pepper and salt. Simmer until the sauce reduces by about half and thickens slightly, stirring occasionally, about 8 minutes.

Meanwhile, bring a large pot of salted water to a boil. Add the fusilli and cook until it is tender but still firm to the bite, stirring occasionally, about 8 minutes. Drain (do not rinse). Add the fusilli and chicken mixture to the Marsala sauce, and toss until the sauce thickens and coats the pasta, about 1 minute.

Divide the pasta among plates. Garnish with thyme sprigs and serve immediately.

COOK'S NOTES: Tossing the fusilli with the Marsala sauce is an important step. It's at this point that the starches and heat from the fusilli continue to thicken the sauce into a silky coating. Because of this, don't rinse the pasta after it's cooked, or reduce the sauce so much that it is already thick before the fusilli is added.

Other pastas, such as penne, rigatoni, and fettuccine, make good substitutes for the fusilli.

Serves 6

SUMAC-COATED CHICKEN KEBAB

THIS INDIAN INSPIRED RECIPE IS A VARIATION TO THE TRADITIONAL KEBAB. THE SPICE COMBINATION IS BOLD AND FLAVORFUL. THE YOGURT ADDS A NICE COATING TO THE CHICKEN AND TENDERIZES THE MEAT AS IT MARINATES. IT'S A CINCH TO PUT TOGETHER AND MAKES A DELICIOUS AND SATISFYING ENTRÉE FOR LUNCH OR DINNER. SERVE THE KEBABS WITH FLUFFY COUSCOUS, TABBOULEH (PAGE 57), OR ROMAINE SALAD WITH HEARTS OF PALM AND ARTICHOKES, (PAGE 64). FOR A HEALTHY ENTRÉE, SERVE THEM ALONGSIDE THE WHEAT BERRY AND GARBANZO BEAN SALAD (PAGE 88).

1/2 cup plain yogurt
1/4 cup chopped fresh Italian parsley
2 tablespoons fresh lemon juice
2 tablespoons paprika
2 tablespoons sumac (page 13)
1 tablespoon minced garlic
1 1/2 teaspoons salt
1 teaspoon ground black pepper
1 teaspoon ground cumin
1/2 teaspoon cayenne pepper
1/2 teaspoon ground nutmeg
2 pounds boneless skinless chicken breasts,
  cut into 2-inch pieces
  Lemon wedges, for garnish
  Mint or Italian parsley for garnish

Stir the yogurt, parsley, lemon juice, paprika, sumac, garlic, salt, black pepper, cumin, cayenne pepper, and nutmeg in a large bowl to blend. Add the chicken and stir to coat completely. Cover and refrigerate at least 1 hour and or up to 1 day, stirring occasionally.

Prepare the barbecue for medium-high heat. Thread the chicken pieces onto 6 metal skewers. Grill the chicken until it is just cooked through and lightly charred on the outside, turning occasionally, about 12 minutes.

Transfer the kebabs to a platter. Garnish with lemon wedges and mint sprigs, and serve.

COOK'S NOTES: You can use lamb or beef instead of chicken, if desired.

Use the leftover grilled chicken in pita bread for a nice sandwich, adding slices of tomatoes and thinly sliced red onions.

Serves 6

BEEF TENDERLOIN WITH SHALLOT AND THYME SAUCE

BEEF TENDERLOIN IS A WONDERFUL ENTRÉE TO SERVE FOR ANY SPECIAL OCCASION. AND SINCE IT CAN BE MADE AHEAD, IT ELIMINATES A FEW LAST MINUTE PREPARATIONS FOR THE HOSTESS. MAKE SURE THE BEEF IS OF GOOD QUALITY. AND USE A COARSELY GROUND BLACK PEPPER SINCE IT IS ONE OF THE ESSENTIAL INGREDIENTS THAT ENHANCES THE FLAVORS OF THE BEEF.

Beef

1 (2 1/2- to 3-pound) beef tenderloin,
   trimmed of fat and sinew
4 tablespoons olive oil
2 tablespoons minced garlic
1 1/2 tablespoons coarsely chopped fresh rosemary
1 teaspoon coarsely ground black pepper
1 teaspoon salt
2 tablespoons Dijon mustard

Sauce

5 tablespoons chilled unsalted butter
1 tablespoon minced garlic
1 tablespoon minced shallot
1 tablespoon chopped fresh thyme
1 3/4 cups beef stock or broth (from one 14-ounce can)
   Ground black pepper, to taste

To make the beef: Tie the beef with kitchen twine to help hold its shape and place it on a heavy baking sheet. Mix 2 tablespoons of oil, garlic, rosemary, pepper and salt, in a small bowl. Rub all but 1 tablespoon of this oil mixture over the beef. Stir the Dijon mustard and 1 tablespoon of oil into the reserved oil mixture in the small bowl. Cover the beef and the mustard mixture separately. Refrigerate at least 2 hours or up to 1 day.

Preheat the oven to 400°F. Heat the remaining 1 tablespoon of oil in a large nonstick skillet over high heat. Add the beef and cook just until brown on all sides, about 5 minutes. Return the beef to the baking sheet (set the skillet aside to use for the sauce; do not clean the skillet).

Spread the mustard mixture over the top of the beef. Roast the beef in the oven to desired doneness, about 30 minutes for medium rare (a meat thermometer will register 130°F when the beef is cooked to medium-rare). Tent the beef with foil to keep it warm.

Meanwhile, prepare the sauce: Discard the oil and any blackened bits on the bottom of the skillet that was used to brown the beef. Melt 1 tablespoon of butter in the same skillet over medium heat. Add the garlic and shallot and sauté until tender, about 1 minute. Stir in the thyme. Add the broth. Bring the broth to a simmer over high heat. Simmer until the liquid is reduced by half, stirring often, about 8 minutes. Remove the skillet from the heat. Whisk in the remaining 4 tablespoons of butter 1 piece at a time, until melted and smooth. Season the sauce to taste with pepper.

Cut the beef crosswise into 1/3-inch-thick slices. Transfer the slices of beef to plates or a platter. Drizzle the sauce over the beef and serve immediately.

COOK'S NOTES: Serve the beef on a bed of braised spinach or with roasted asparagus, and potato gratin or mashed potatoes with mushroom sauce. To complete a colorful dinner plate, serve teardrop tomatoes tossed with olive oil and basil.

The beef can be seared a day before serving. After it is seared, spread the mustard mixture over it, then cover and refrigerate. To serve, just pop it in the oven to bake.

This roast has so many variations. The Pomegranate Sauce (page 155) complements the beef well, too; make it instead of the sauce used here, if desired. You can cut any leftover beef into thin slices and use it in a sandwich with avocado slices and tomatoes on whole-grain bread, or serve it atop a summer salad drizzled with Balsamic Pomegranate Vinaigrette (page 92).

Serves 6

CHICKEN WITH MUSHROOMS, OLIVES, CAPERS, AND TOMATOES

THE MUSHROOMS, OLIVES AND THE CAPERS TASTE GREAT TOGETHER IN THIS SUCCULENT CHICKEN DISH. FOR A QUICK AND DELICIOUS DINNER, SERVE IT WITH A MIXED BABY GREEN SALAD DRIZZLED WITH LEMON JUICE AND OLIVE OIL, AND SLICES OF WARM CRUSTY BREAD.

2 pounds boneless skinless chicken thighs
2 teaspoons ground black pepper
1 3/4 teaspoons salt
4 tablespoons olive oil
1 1/2 pounds fresh assorted mushrooms
  (such as cremini, oyster, and
  stemmed shiitake), sliced
1 (14-ounce) can chicken broth
3/4 cup pitted Kalamata olives
2 tablespoons drained capers
2 tablespoons minced garlic
2 tablespoons minced shallots
3 tablespoons unsalted butter
3 plum tomatoes, seeded and diced
1 cup red and yellow teardrop tomatoes
1/3 cup pine nuts, toasted (page 18)
3 tablespoons chopped fresh Italian parsley

In a large bowl, sprinkle the chicken with 3/4 teaspoon each of pepper and salt. Heat 2 tablespoons of oil in a heavy large skillet over high heat. Working in 2 batches, add the chicken and cook until golden brown, just cooked through, about 3 minutes per side. Transfer the chicken to a platter and cover it with foil to keep it warm.

Meanwhile, heat the remaining 2 tablespoons of oil in the same skillet over high heat. Add the mushrooms and sauté until they are pale golden, about 8 minutes. Pour in the broth and simmer for 2 minutes. Add the olives, capers, garlic, shallots, and remaining salt and pepper. Sauté until the sauce reduces by about half, about 3 minutes. Stir in the butter one piece at a time. Just before serving, add the plum tomatoes and teardrop tomatoes. Decrease the heat to low and cook just until the tomatoes are heated through, but not soft, about 1 minute.

Spoon the sauce over the chicken. Sprinkle with the pine nuts and parsley, and serve.

COOK'S NOTES: If using chicken breast make sure they are cooked 3 minutes longer than cooking the chicken thighs. The breasts meat is usually much thicker and larger.

Serves 6

BEEF AND RICE
STUFFED VEGETABLES

THE ORIGIN OF THIS STUFFED VEGETABLE
RECIPE IS NOT CLEAR; EACH OF THE MIDDLE
EASTERN COUNTRIES CLAIMS IT IS THEIR OWN
CREATION. USUALLY SERVED AT ELABORATE
BANQUETS AND LARGE FAMILY GATHERINGS.
THE VARIETY OF COLORS, TEXTURES, AND
FLAVORS THAT THIS DISH OFFERS MAKES IT
A POPULAR ONE. TO GET THE OPTIMUM TASTE,
IT IS IMPORTANT TO SERVE THE STUFFED
VEGETABLES HOT. (IT TASTES EVEN BETTER
THE NEXT DAY!)

Beef Filling

1 pound lean ground beef
3 cups finely chopped onion
1 1/2 cups uncooked short-grained white rice
1 cup finely chopped green bell pepper
1 (6-ounce) can tomato paste
1/2 cup chopped fresh Italian parsley
1/4 cup chopped fresh mint
1/4 cup fresh lemon juice
2 tablespoons chopped fresh basil
2 tablespoons crushed dried mint
2 tablespoons minced garlic
4 teaspoons salt
1 teaspoon dried crushed red pepper
1 teaspoon ground black pepper
2 cups finely chopped tomatoes

Vegetables

1 green cabbage, cored
7 Japanese eggplants, halved lengthwise
2 zucchini, halved lengthwise
2 yellow crookneck squash, halved lengthwise
3 small red bell peppers, halved crosswise

Broth

3 tablespoons butter
2 tablespoons minced garlic
1 tablespoon crushed dried mint
1/4 cup tomato paste
2 cups water
1/4 cup fresh lemon juice
  Tzatziki Sauce (recipe follows)

To make the beef filling: Stir all of the ingredients
except the tomatoes in a large bowl to blend. Gently
mix in the tomatoes. Cover and refrigerate until
ready to use.

To prepare the vegetables: Bring a large pot of salted
water to a boil. Add the whole head of cabbage and cook
until the cabbage leaves are wilted and start to fall off
of the cabbage head, about 3 minutes. The goal is to wilt
the cabbage so that the leaves will roll easily. Carefully
remove the leaves with tongs without tearing them,
and set them in a colander to drain. Cool slightly.

Reserve the 8 largest cabbage leaves. Line a heavy
large roasting pan with the remaining cabbage leaves.
Cut the reserved 8 leaves in half and trim away the large
center vein. Place 2 tablespoons of filling at one short
end of each halved cabbage leaf. Roll up the leaf tightly
as you would a cigar, folding in the ends and enclosing
the filling completely. Repeat with the remaining halved
cabbage leaves. Arrange the stuffed cabbage in the
roasting pan atop the bed of cabbage leaves.

Using a small sharp knife, carefully shave away
the inner flesh of eggplants, yellow squash, zucchini
and bell peppers, leaving about 1/8-inch thick shells.
Be careful not to pierce through the skin. Spoon the
filling into each halved eggplants, yellow squash,
zucchini, and bell peppers. Arrange the stuffed
vegetables in the roasting pan alongside the
stuffed cabbage.

To make the broth: Preheat the oven to 350°F. Melt the butter in a heavy medium saucepan over medium-high heat until it foams and starts to sizzle. Stir in the garlic and mint. Whisk in the tomato paste. Add the water and lemon juice. Bring the mixture to a boil. Pour the hot broth over the vegetables. Cover the roasting pan tightly with foil.

Transfer the roasting pan to the oven and bake until the broth has evaporated, the rice in the filling is tender, and the vegetables are tender, about 1 hour.

Transfer the stuffed vegetables to a large serving platter. Serve hot with the Tzatziki Sauce.

COOK'S NOTES: You can use other summer squash, such as chayote squash, which are available at Latin American markets. Chayote squash are pale green, about 2 to 3-inches long, and about 1 1/2 inches in diameter. They weigh about 2 1/2 ounces each and are egg-shaped.

If you don't have a roasting pan large enough to fit all the vegetables, use two baking dishes instead.

Serves 6 to 8 servings

TZATZIKI SAUCE

A FLAVORFUL AND VERSATILE CUCUMBER SAUCE THAT IS OFTEN MADE WITH YOGURT OR A COMBINATION OF SOUR CREAM AND YOGURT. IT ACCOMPANIES SALADS, VEGETABLES, OR SANDWICHES. IT IS A TERRIFIC DIPPING SAUCE FOR VARIETY OF LAMB DISHES AS WELL AS GRILLED FOODS.

1 1/2 cups plain yogurt
1/2 large hothouse cucumber, finely diced
1 teaspoon dried mint, crumbled
1 teaspoon salt
1/2 teaspoon garlic powder

Stir the yogurt, cucumber, mint, salt, and garlic powder in a medium bowl to blend.

COOK'S NOTES: The sauce will keep up to 2 days. Store it in a glass jar with a tight-fitting lid and keep it refrigerated.

Makes about 2 cups

ROSEMARY-GARLIC CHICKEN WITH LEMON

CHICKEN WITH ROSEMARY IS A MATCH MADE IN HEAVEN. SERVE THIS DISH WITH YOUR FAVORITE GRILLED VEGETABLES SUCH AS ASPARAGUS, ZUCCHINI, YELLOW CROOKNECK SQUASH, AND RED BELL PEPPERS. THE ROASTED POTATOES WITH PARSLEY AND THYME (PAGE 140) OR THE EGGPLANT TAGINE (PAGE 139) MAKE DELICIOUS SIDE DISHES, TOO.

3 tablespoons fresh lemon juice
2 tablespoons minced garlic
1 tablespoon chopped fresh rosemary
1 tablespoon chopped fresh thyme
1 tablespoon salt
1/2 teaspoon ground black pepper
1/4 cup plus 2 tablespoons olive oil
8 boneless chicken breasts (with skin on)
  Italian parsley or rosemary sprigs, for garnish
  Lemon wedges, for garnish

Whisk the lemon juice, garlic, rosemary, thyme, salt, pepper, and 1/4 cup of oil in a large bowl to blend. Add the chicken and toss well to coat. Cover and refrigerate, tossing occasionally, for at least 1 hour or up to 2 days.

Prepare the barbecue for medium-high heat. Grill the chicken breasts until they are just cooked through and golden brown, about 4 minutes per side. Transfer the chicken to a platter. Garnish with the parsley or rosemary sprigs and lemon wedges.

COOK'S NOTES: When grilling the chicken, position the rack fairly close to the heat source to help seal in the juices that keep the chicken tender and succulent. A chicken breast is cooked perfectly when it reaches 160°F (use an instant-read meat thermometer). If you exceed that temperature, the chicken is considered over-cooked and will mostly likely yield a stringy or rubbery texture.

The marinated chicken is also delicious when broiled.

Try using bold flavors in your marinade such as lime juice, more garlic, or more fresh thyme.

Serves 8

MOUSSAKA

MOUSSAKA IS OFTEN REGARDED AS THE GREEK VERSION OF SHEPHERD'S PIE OR LASAGNA. THE DELICIOUS COMBINATION OF EGGPLANT, SPICED MEAT SAUCE, AND MELTING CHEESES HAS ALSO MADE IT ONE OF THE WORLD'S CLASSIC DISHES. RICH AND HEARTY, IT IS A WONDERFUL DISH TO SERVE AT A CASUAL PARTY. OFFER IT WITH CLASSIC RICE PILAF (PAGE 133) AND ROMAINE SALAD WITH HEARTS OF PALM AND ARTICHOKES (PAGE 64).

2/3 cup olive oil
1 1/2 pounds lean ground beef (7% fat)
1 small onion, finely chopped
1 tablespoon minced garlic
1 (6-ounce) can tomato paste
1 (28-ounce) can diced tomatoes with juices
1/2 cup dry white wine
1 1/2 teaspoons salt, plus more to taste
1 teaspoon ground black pepper, plus more to taste
1 teaspoon dried oregano
1/2 teaspoon ground allspice
1/2 teaspoon ground cinnamon
1/2 teaspoon ground nutmeg
1/8 teaspoon dried crushed red pepper
1/4 cup finely chopped fresh Italian parsley
3 1/2 cups Béchamel Sauce (recipe follows)
  Nonstick cooking spray
3 large eggplants (about 1 pound each),
  cut crosswise into 1/2-inch-thick rounds
1 tablespoon butter
1 1/2 cups freshly grated Parmesan cheese
3 large eggs

Heat 1/3 cup of oil in a heavy large skillet over medium-high heat. Add the beef and sauté until lightly browned, breaking up the beef with the back of a wooden spoon, about 8 minutes. Decrease the heat to medium. Add the onion and sauté until it is tender, about 8 minutes. Stir in the garlic, then the tomato paste. Add the diced tomatoes, wine, 1 1/2 teaspoons of salt, 1 teaspoon of black pepper, the oregano, allspice, cinnamon, nutmeg, and crushed red pepper. Simmer uncovered until the sauce thickens, stirring occasionally, about 20 minutes. Let the meat sauce cool to lukewarm, then stir in the parsley and 1 cup of Béchamel Sauce.

Meanwhile, preheat the oven to 400°F. Line 2 large baking sheets with foil. Spray the foil with nonstick cooking spray. Arrange the eggplant slices in a single layer over the baking sheets. Brush the remaining 1/3 cup of oil over both sides of the eggplant slices. Sprinkle the eggplant with salt and pepper. Bake until the eggplant slices are tender and golden brown, about 12 minutes per side. Set aside to cool.

Butter the bottom and sides of a 13x9x2-inch baking dish. Arrange one third of the eggplant slices over the bottom of the dish. Sprinkle 1/2 cup of Parmesan cheese over the eggplant. Spread half of the meat sauce (about 3 cups) over the cheese. Spread 1 cup of the Béchamel Sauce over. Repeat layering the eggplant slices, Parmesan cheese, and meat sauce one more time. Cover with the remaining eggplant slices.

Whisk the 3 eggs and remaining 1 1/2 cups of Béchamel Sauce in a medium bowl to blend. Pour the sauce over the moussaka. Sprinkle with the remaining 1/2 cup of Parmesan cheese. Bake uncovered until the moussaka is golden brown on top and the sauce bubbles, about 45 minutes. Let the moussaka stand for 15 minutes to set up slightly before serving.

COOK'S NOTES: The moussaka can be assembled
1 day ahead, then baked just before serving.
After it is baked, it will keep for 2 days, covered
and refrigerated. To rewarm the moussaka, cover
with foil and bake it in the oven until it is heated
through or you can microwave it.

Instead of dried oregano, you can use fresh oregano
or fresh thyme.

You can make the dish vegetarian by omitting the
meat from the sauce, and using about 1 cup of ricotta
cheese and extra Parmesan cheese. When layering,
spread the ricotta cheese over the eggplant slices before
the Parmesan cheese and sauce are added.

Make sure you have the roasted eggplant, the meat
sauce, and Béchamel Sauce ready before assembling
the moussaka

Serves 8

BÉCHAMEL SAUCE

3 tablespoons unsalted butter
1/3 cup all purpose flour
3 1/2 cups whole milk, warmed
3/4 teaspoon salt
1/8 teaspoon ground nutmeg
1/16 teaspoon ground white pepper

Melt the butter in a heavy large saucepan over medium-
low heat. Add the flour and whisk for 3 minutes.
Whisk in the milk. Increase the heat to medium-high.
Whisk the sauce until it comes to a simmer and is
thick and smooth, about 3 minutes. Whisk in the
salt, nutmeg, and white pepper.

Makes 3 1/2 cups

PHYLLO PURSES WITH CHICKEN AND CARAMELIZED ONIONS

THE HERBS AND MUSHROOMS EXPLODE
WITH FLAVOR IN THIS ELEGANT DISH, AND
THE CARAMELIZED ONIONS LEND A HINT
OF SWEETNESS. YOU CAN MAKE THE PURSES
AHEAD OF TIME THEN JUST BAKE THEM
RIGHT BEFORE SERVING (SEE COOK'S NOTES).
CHICKEN NEVER LOOKED OR TASTED SO GOOD!

Filling

5 tablespoons olive oil
1 onion, thinly sliced
2 boneless skinless chicken breasts
1 teaspoon ground black pepper
1 teaspoon salt
1 tablespoon minced shallots
2 teaspoons minced garlic
6 ounces shiitake mushrooms, stemmed and sliced
1/2 cup thinly sliced fresh spinach leaves
1/2 cup pine nuts, toasted (page 18)
4 ounces Haloume cheese, shredded (see cook's notes)
3 ounces sun-dried tomatoes,
  soaked in hot water for 30 minutes,
  drained and sliced
2 ounces feta cheese, crumbled
10 pitted Kalamata olives, sliced
2 tablespoons chopped fresh chives
2 tablespoons chopped fresh Italian parsley
1 tablespoon chopped fresh thyme

Purses

12 sheets frozen phyllo dough, thawed
1/2 cup (1 stick) unsalted butter, melted
  Mushroom, Tomato, and White Wine Sauce
  (recipe follows)
  Italian parsley sprigs, for garnish
  Chopped fresh chives, for garnish

To make the filling: Heat 2 tablespoons of oil in a heavy large nonstick skillet over medium-high heat. Add the onion slices and sauté until golden brown, about 10 minutes. Remove the skillet from the heat. Using a slotted spoon, transfer the onions to a large bowl.

Heat 1 tablespoon of oil in the same skillet over medium-high heat. Sprinkle the chicken with 1/2 teaspoon each of pepper and salt. Cook the chicken until it is golden brown and just cooked through, about 4 minutes per side. Transfer the chicken to a plate and cool.

Heat the remaining 2 tablespoons of oil in the same skillet over medium heat. Add the shallots and garlic, and sauté until fragrant, about 30 seconds. Increase the heat to medium-high. Add the mushrooms and sauté until they are tender and beginning to brown, about 5 minutes. Add the mushroom mixture to the caramelized onions in the large bowl. Cool completely.

Cut the chicken into 1/2-inch pieces then add it to the mushroom mixture. Stir in the spinach, pine nuts, Haloume cheese, sun-dried tomatoes, feta cheese, olives, chives, parsley, thyme, and remaining 1/2 teaspoon of each salt and pepper. (The filling can be prepared 1 day ahead. Cover and refrigerate.)

To make the purses: Preheat the oven to 350°F. Line a heavy large baking sheet with parchment paper. Unroll the phyllo sheets on a dry flat surface. Carefully remove 1 sheet of phyllo and lay it on a work surface (keep the remaining phyllo covered with plastic wrap and a damp kitchen towel). Brush the phyllo sheet with some melted butter. Fold the phyllo to form a 13 by 81/2-inch rectangle. Brush more butter over the phyllo. Mound 1/2 cup of filling in the center of the phyllo rectangle. Gather the corners of the phyllo together over the filling, forming a purse. Twist the ends closed. Brush the purse with melted butter and place it on the prepared baking sheet. Repeat with the remaining phyllo sheets and filling, forming 12 purses total. Bake the purses until they are golden brown, about 30 minutes.

Place the purses in the center of 12 plates. Spoon the Mushroom, Tomato and White Wine Sauce around the purses. Garnish with parsley sprigs and chives, and serve.

COOK'S NOTES: You can freeze the stuffed phyllo purses in an airtight container up to 1 week. Then, when you're ready to serve, just place the frozen purses on a baking sheet and bake as directed above (the frozen purses take a few minutes longer to bake than those at room temperature).

The filling can also be wrapped with the phyllo sheets to form bundles. To form them into bundles, mound 1/2 cup of the filling atop the bottom third of the folded phyllo sheet. Roll up the phyllo to enclose the filling completely as for a burrito. Butter the seam and place the pastries seam side down on the baking sheets.

Haloume is a white semi-hard cheese made of 100% sheep's milk and melts beautifully when used in pressed sandwiches. It is delicious in omelets and in salads, or served alone as an appetizer with a bowl of olives and pita bread. Feta cheese is a good substitute for Haloume.

Serves 12

MUSHROOM, TOMATO, AND WHITE WINE SAUCE

A DELICIOUS SAUCE THAT IS EASY TO PREPARE AND CAN BE USED ON A VARIETY OF GRILLED OR SAUTÉED FOODS. I LOVE USING THIS SAUCE ON GRILLED HALIBUT, SALMON, OR A WHITE FLESHED DELICATE FISH.

3 tablespoons olive oil
2 tablespoons finely chopped shallots
2 tablespoons minced garlic
1 1/2 pounds sliced assorted mushrooms
  (such as oyster, cremini, and stemmed shiitake)
1 1/2 cups chicken broth
1 1/2 cups dry white wine
3 plum tomatoes, seeded and diced
3/4 teaspoon ground black pepper
3/4 teaspoon salt
6 tablespoons (3/4 stick) cold unsalted butter,
  cut into 6 pieces
4 ounces cherry tomatoes (about 1 cup), halved

Heat the oil in a heavy large skillet over medium heat. Add the shallots and garlic and sauté until tender, about 1 minute. Add the mushrooms. Increase the heat to medium-high and sauté until the mushrooms are tender and golden brown, about 8 minutes. Stir in the broth and wine and bring to a boil. Add the plum tomatoes. Decrease the heat to medium and simmer until the liquid reduces by half, about 10 minutes. Mix in the pepper and salt. Add the butter 1 piece at a time, stirring until melted and well blended before adding the next piece. Stir in the cherry tomatoes.

COOK'S NOTES: This versatile sauce goes well spooned over most grilled chicken or fish. Try it with pasta or rice, too.

Makes 5 cups

SEAFOOD

Cooking seafood is all about freshness and timing. These delicious seafood recipes, derived from traditional Mediterranean cuisine, require only minimum cooking. They're easy and so satisfying.

MOROCCO 1998

How to describe the busy Moroccan markets? Imagine
a fixed parade of vibrant colors, endless aisles of painted
stalls roofed by cloth swathes of all hues. The white sun
illuminates the entire scene. The aisles' shade offers
little respite as crowds fill the passageways, buying
and selling. Yet we hardly notice the heat. We're too
distracted by the exciting din of commerce and the
riches being sold: golden, rose-tinted apples; shining
green, yellow and red peppers; baton-shaped sausages;
and all kinds of meats, chicken and smoked fish
hanging whole on long lines. And the spices! Barrels
and jars full of powders the colors of fiery sunsets.
Their pungent fragrance floats among us.

I first visited Morocco in 1998, on a culinary trip
with famed cookbook author and teacher Kitty Morse.
There I learned the magic of sauces, like the amazing
Charmoula that uniquely and evocatively employ
Moroccan spices—spices readily available to the
American cook. The recipes I learned in Morocco
delighted me so much, as soon as I tried them I faxed
them to the chef at my restaurant back home so he
could begin experimenting with them. Thus was born
the Moroccan Salmon, a dish that has become one
of the Bistro's most popular.

GRILLED MOROCCAN SALMON WITH CHARMOULA SAUCE

NOT LONG AGO, EVERYONE STARTED TALKING ABOUT THE CURATIVE QUALITIES OF OMEGA-3 FATTY ACIDS, THE KIND PREVALENT IN FISH. SINCE THEN, THIS PARTICULAR SALMON ENTRÉE HAS BECOME ONE OF OUR BIGGEST SELLERS AT THE BISTRO. CHARMOULA IS A TRADITIONAL MOROCCAN MARINADE USUALLY MADE UP OF WARM SPICES SUCH AS CUMIN, PAPRIKA, GARLIC, AND CINNAMON. IT'S USED FOR MEATS, SEAFOOD, POULTRY, OR VEGETABLES. THE EXOTIC FLAVOR OF THE MOROCCAN SPICES THAT SEASONS THE SALMON AND SAUCE IN THIS RECIPE WILL SURELY INTRIGUE YOUR DINNER GUESTS. IT'S HARD TO PIN DOWN JUST WHAT SPICES YOU TASTE, BUT IT'S FUN TO TRY!

Salmon

6 (6-ounces each) boneless skinless salmon fillets
1/2 teaspoon ground black pepper
1/2 teaspoon salt
1/3 cup Moroccan Spices (recipe follows)
3 tablespoons olive oil

Charmoula Sauce

1/4 cup olive oil
1/4 cup finely chopped shallots
1 tablespoon minced garlic
1 1/2 pounds plum tomatoes (about 9),
  seeded and finely diced
3/4 cup chopped fresh cilantro
3 tablespoons fresh lemon juice
1 teaspoon Moroccan Spices
1 teaspoon salt
3/4 teaspoon ground black pepper
  Cilantro sprigs, for garnish

To make the salmon: Preheat the oven to 350°F. Sprinkle the salmon with black pepper and salt. Place 1/3 cup of the Moroccan Spices on a plate. Dredge the salmon in the spices to generously coat the top and bottom (do not coat the sides of the salmon).

Heat 3 tablespoons of oil on a large griddle over medium-high heat. Cook the salmon fillets just until golden brown, about 1 minute per side. Using a metal spatula, transfer the fillets to a heavy large rimmed baking sheet. Bake just until the fillets are cooked through, about 5 minutes.

Meanwhile, prepare the charmoula sauce: Heat the 1/4 cup of the oil in a heavy large skillet over medium-high heat. Add the shallots and garlic and sauté until tender, about 1 minute. Add the tomatoes, cilantro, lemon juice, Moroccan Spices, salt, and pepper. Sauté just until the tomatoes release their juices but they still hold their shape, about 1 minute.

Place the salmon fillets on warm plates and spoon the sauce over. Garnish with cilantro sprigs and serve.

COOK'S NOTES: Make sure you don't overcook the salmon; it should be just flaky.

Mashed potatoes and braised fresh spinach make good accompaniments to the salmon.

Serves 6

MOROCCAN SPICES

THE COMBINATION OF THESE SPICES ARE
CONSIDERED IN THE FAMILY OF WARM SPICES.
THIS SEASONING BLENDS BEAUTIFULLY WITH
SOUPS, SALADS, SEAFOOD, CHICKEN, OR ANY
OTHER MEATS.

3 tablespoons paprika
2 tablespoons dried thyme
2 tablespoons ground cumin
1 tablespoon grated nutmeg
1 tablespoon ground black pepper
1 tablespoon ground ginger
2 teaspoons ground cinnamon
1 teaspoon cayenne pepper
1 teaspoon ground allspice

Stir all the ingredients in a small bowl to blend.
Transfer to a jar and seal with the lid. Refrigerate up
to 1 week.

Makes 3/4 cup

SCALLOPS AND SHRIMP WITH LINGUINE

SERVE THIS PASTA WITH CRUSTY FRENCH BREAD, THE ROMAINE SALAD WITH HEARTS OF PALM AND ARTICHOKES, (PAGE 64), AND A CHILLED WHITE WINE SUCH AS PINOT GRIGIO OR CHARDONNAY.

4 tablespoons olive oil
8 ounces assorted fresh mushrooms (such as cremini, baby portabella, and stemmed shiitake), sliced
2 pounds plum tomatoes, seeded and chopped
3/4 cup plus 2 tablespoons chopped fresh Italian parsley
3/4 cup chopped fresh basil
1/2 cup Basic Tomato Herb Sauce (page 142)
1 tablespoon minced garlic
1 1/4 teaspoons ground black pepper, plus more to taste
1 1/4 teaspoons salt, plus more to taste
1/4 teaspoon dried crushed red pepper (optional)
18 sea scallops
18 jumbo shrimp, peeled and deveined
12 ounces dried linguine
8 ounces feta cheese, crumbled
1/2 cup freshly grated Parmesan cheese

Heat 2 tablespoons of oil in a deep large nonstick frying pan over medium-high heat. Add the mushrooms and sauté until tender and beginning to brown, about 8 minutes. Stir in the tomatoes, 3/4 cup of parsley, basil, Basic Tomato Herb Sauce, garlic, 3/4 teaspoon each of black pepper and salt and the crushed red pepper. Cook until the sauce is heated through but the tomatoes still hold their shape, stirring often, about 5 minutes. Cover the sauce and set it aside.

Pat the scallops and shrimp with paper towels to dry. Sprinkle with the remaining 1/2 teaspoon of each black pepper and salt. Heat the remaining 2 tablespoons of oil in a heavy large skillet over medium-high heat. Add the scallops and cook until brown and just opaque in the center, about 2 minutes per side. Transfer the scallops to a plate and tent with foil to keep warm. Add the shrimp to the same skillet and sauté just until pink and cooked through, about 3 minutes. Be careful not to overcook the scallops or shrimp, as they will become rubbery.

Meanwhile, bring a large pot of salted water to a boil. Add the linguine and cook until it is tender but still firm to the bite, stirring often, about 8 minutes. Drain the linguine (do not rinse) and toss it with the sauce, feta cheese, Parmesan cheese, scallops, and shrimp. Season the pasta to taste with more salt and black pepper.

Divide the pasta among 6 plates. Sprinkle with the remaining 2 tablespoons of parsley and serve.

COOK'S NOTES: For maximum flavor and perfect texture, cook the pasta just before serving.

The Basic Tomato Herb Sauce adds a wonderful depth of flavor to the dish. If you don't have time to make it, use your favorite marinara sauce instead

Serves 6

SALMON PLAKI WITH VEGETABLES AND WHITE BEANS

SALMON IS A MILD FLAVORED FISH, HIGH IN NUTRIENTS, AND SUITABLE TO AN ARRAY OF COOKING METHODS. HERE, IT'S USED IN A GREEK STEW, CALLED PLAKI, WITH WHITE BEANS, VEGETABLES, AND A SPICY TOMATO SAUCE. IT IS DELICIOUS WITH STEAMED RICE AND BRAISED SPINACH OR KALE, AND A LOVELY CHILLED SEMI-SWEET WHITE WINE.

3 red bell peppers, roasted, peeled and seeded
2 tablespoons chili garlic sauce
2 tablespoons tomato paste
6 (6-ounces each) boneless skinless salmon fillets
1 1/4 teaspoons ground black pepper
1 1/4 teaspoons salt
3 tablespoons olive oil
1 cup medium diced peeled carrots
1 cup medium diced celery
1 cup medium diced peeled russet potatoes
4 teaspoons minced garlic
1 (15-ounce) can Great Northern beans,
  drained and rinsed
1 1/4 cups clam juice
1/2 cup chopped fresh Italian parsley

Roast the peppers over a gas flame until lightly charred all over, about 10 minutes. Enclose the peppers in a plastic bag until cool enough to handle. Peel, seed, and slice the peppers into 1/4-inch-wide strips. Pat the peppers dry to remove any excess liquid.

Puree the roasted peppers, chili garlic sauce, and tomato paste in a food processor until almost smooth. Sprinkle the salmon with 1/2 teaspoon of each black pepper and salt. Spoon 1 tablespoon of the red pepper sauce over the top of each salmon fillet.

Heat the oil in a heavy large skillet over medium-high heat. Add the carrots, celery, and potatoes, and sauté until the vegetables are crisp-tender and beginning to brown, about 8 minutes. Stir in the garlic, then the beans, clam juice, parsley, and remaining red pepper sauce. Bring to a simmer. Decrease the heat to medium-low. Cover and simmer until the vegetables are tender, about 5 minutes. Stir in the remaining 3/4 teaspoon of each black pepper and. Arrange the salmon atop of the vegetable mixture. Cover and simmer gently over medium-low heat until the fish is firm to the touch and just cooked through, about 12 minutes.

COOK'S NOTES: Chili garlic sauce is available in the Asian foods section of most supermarkets. The taste is pungent and adds a wonderful zip to the food.

Serves 6

PAN-SEARED WHITEFISH WITH TOMATO CURRY

THIS IS AN ADAPTATION OF AN IRAQI NATIONAL DISH CALLED "MAZGOOF." THE CURRY IS AN ESSENTIAL INGREDIENT, BUT IT IS SUBTLE. YOU CAN USE ANY MILD WHITE-FLESHED FISH SUCH AS HALIBUT, OR STRIPED BASS. JUST BE SURE THE FISH IS MILD ENOUGH SO THAT IS DOES NOT OVERPOWER THE DELICIOUS SAUCE. THE BEST WAY TO SERVE THIS DISH IS WITH SIMPLE STEAMED BASMATI RICE OR CLASSIC RICE PILAF (PAGE 133), WHICH WON'T COMPETE WITH THE FLAVORFUL SAUCE.

6 (6-ounces each) center-cut whitefish
  fillets with skin (about 1 inch thick)
1 3/4 teaspoons salt
3/4 teaspoon ground black pepper
4 tablespoons olive oil
2 tablespoons unsalted butter
2 medium onions, thinly sliced
3 tablespoons mild red Indian
  curry paste (see Cook's Notes)
2 tablespoons minced garlic
5 ripe tomatoes, peeled, seeded and
  coarsely chopped (see Cook's Notes)
1/2 cup plus 2 tablespoons chopped fresh Italian parsley
2 tablespoons fresh lemon juice
  Lemon wedges, for garnish
  Italian parsley sprigs, for garnish

Preheat the oven to 350°F. Sprinkle the fish with 1/2 teaspoon each of salt and black pepper. Heat 1 tablespoon of oil in a heavy large skillet over medium-high heat. Place 3 fish fillets, skin side down, in the skillet and cook until the skin is crisp and deep golden, about 5 minutes. Using a large metal spatula, transfer the fish, skin side up, to a heavy large rimmed baking sheet (the fish will not be cooked through at this point). Repeat with the remaining fish fillets.

Pour off the used oil in the skillet. Melt the butter with the remaining 3 tablespoons of oil in the same skillet over medium-high heat. Add the onions and sauté until they are translucent, about 8 minutes. Stir in the curry paste and garlic, then the tomatoes. Simmer until the tomatoes release their juices and become very tender, stirring frequently, about 2 minutes. Stir in 1/2 cup of parsley and lemon juice. Season the curry sauce to taste with the remaining 1 1/4 teaspoons of salt and 1/4 teaspoon of black pepper.

Meanwhile, bake the fish until it is just cooked through, about 5 minutes (do not overcook the fish as it will turn tough and rubbery). Transfer the fish to plates and spoon the curry sauce over. Sprinkle with the remaining 2 tablespoons of parsley. Garnish with lemon wedges and parsley sprigs, and serve.

COOK'S NOTES: For this recipe, use an Indian red curry paste rather than a Thai red curry paste. Both are exotic and delicious, but the blends of spices are different and lend very distinct flavors. You can find wonderful Indian curry pastes at Indian market and most supermarket and specialty foods stores. "If curry pastes is not available, substitute with 1 teaspoon of curry powder."

Curry powder is a blend of up to twenty spices that generally includes cumin, coriander, red chilies, turmeric, and fenugreek. The mixture varies in strength and potency and is generally sold as either mild or hot. Curry paste is the combination of curry powder, ghee (clarified butter), and other seasonings. There really is no substitute for its deep, earthy flavor. I suggest using the mild curry for this recipe. Curry pastes are widely available at most supermarkets, but the best types are found at Asian or Indian markets where they are also the freshest quality.

To peel the tomatoes, simply drop them into a saucepan of boiling water for 20 seconds, then set them aside until they are cool enough to handle. The skins will peel off easily.

Serves 6

SALMON BURGER WITH AVOCADO-LIME GUACAMOLE

EVER SINCE THE CRAZE FOR HIGH PROTEIN FOODS BEGAN, I'VE BEEN COMPELLED TO COME UP WITH A VARIETY OF NEW MENU SELECTIONS. ALONG THE WAY, I DISCOVERED HOW WELL SALMON WORKS AS A BURGER! THE COMBINATION OF ASIAN INGREDIENTS AND FRESH HERBS BALANCE THE BURGER BEAUTIFULLY. I LOVE IT ON A BUN, BUT IF YOU'RE KEEPING A LOW-CARB LIFESTYLE, YOU CAN FORGO THE BUN AND TOP THE BURGER WITH THE AVOCADO-LIME GUACAMOLE AND SERVE THE CABBAGE SALAD WITH MINT AND CILANTRO ON THE SIDE. IF YOU PREFER, WRAP THE BURGER WITH LETTUCE LEAVES IN PLACE OF THE BUN.

1 1/2 pounds boneless skinless salmon fillet, minced by hand
1/2 cup mayonnaise
1/4 cup minced shallots
3 tablespoons coarsely chopped fresh cilantro
3 tablespoons finely chopped fresh chives
3 tablespoons finely chopped fresh dill
3 tablespoons minced green onions
3 tablespoons minced lemongrass (from 1 stalk)
3 tablespoons minced peeled fresh ginger
3 tablespoons thinly sliced fresh mint leaves
2 tablespoons fish sauce (nam pla)
2 tablespoons hot chili sauce (such as Sriracha)
1 tablespoon minced garlic
1 teaspoon salt
1/2 teaspoon ground black pepper
1 1/2 cups panko (Japanese breadcrumbs)
1/2 cup raw sesame seeds
2 tablespoons (or more) vegetable oil
6 onion hamburger buns, split
  Avocado-Lime Guacamole (recipe follows)
  Cabbage Salad with Mint and Cilantro (page 90)

Stir the first 15 ingredients in a large bowl just until blended (do not overwork the fish). Stir in 1 cup of panko. Form the salmon mixture into six 4 1/2-inch-diameter patties that are 1/2-inch-thick. Cover and refrigerate at least 2 hours and up to 1 day.

Stir the sesame seeds with the remaining 1/2 cup of panko in a shallow bowl. Generously coat the patties with the sesame mixture. Heat 2 tablespoons of oil on a large nonstick griddle over medium-high heat. Working in batches, grill the patties until golden brown on the outside and just cooked through, about 3 minutes per side, adding more oil to the griddle as needed.

Generously spread the Avocado-Lime Guacamole over the bun bottoms. Place the salmon patties on the bun bottoms. Top with the Cabbage Salad with Mint and Cilantro (page 90) and serve with bun tops.

COOK'S NOTES: Do not use a food processor to mince the salmon. The food processor tends to make the fish stringy and mushy. Instead, use a large sharp knife.

Panko are the Japanese breadcrumbs found in Asian markets, natural foods stores, specialty markets and some supermarkets. If panko is not available, use unseasoned breadcrumbs instead.

To reduce the fat and calories, use soft silken tofu or sour cream instead of mayonnaise. You can also use round ciabatta, focaccia, hamburger buns, round sourdough, or pita bread. Additional toppings for the salmon burger include daikon sprouts and, for color and texture, seeded and cored tomatoes cut into julienne strips.

Serves 6

AVOCADO-LIME GUACAMOLE

THIS IS ONE OF MY FAVORITE DIPS. I LIKE
TO SPOON IT ATOP THE SALMON BURGER
AND WITH CRAB CAKES, GRILLED CHICKEN
OR FISH, AND OF COURSE, CORN TORTILLA
CHIPS. PARMESAN CHEESE IS THE SECRET
INGREDIENT. IT ADDS BALANCE AND FLAVOR
TO THE AVOCADOS, CREATING A UNIQUE
GUACAMOLE.

3 ripe avocados, peeled, pitted, and cubed
1/2 cup sour cream
3 tablespoons chopped fresh basil
3 tablespoons finely chopped shallots
2 tablespoons freshly grated Parmesan cheese
2 tablespoons fresh lemon juice
2 tablespoons fresh lime juice
2 tablespoons minced garlic
1 serrano chili, seeded and minced
1 teaspoon ground black pepper
1 teaspoon salt

Using a potato masher or a large fork, coarsely mash all
the ingredients in a large bowl. Serve immediately.

COOK'S NOTES: Guacamole is best served immediately
after it's made, but if necessary, this one can be made
up to 8 hours ahead. To keep it as fresh as possible,
place a piece of plastic wrap directly on the guacamole
to prevent it from discoloring, then refrigerate it.
Just before serving, stir the guacamole to blend.

Makes 2 1/2 cups

SESAME-CRUSTED SALMON SALAD

TO PROMOTE GOOD HEALTH, PAPAYA HAS BECOME POPULAR WITH CHEFS ALL AROUND THE COUNTRY. TROPICAL FRUITS OFFER FLAVOR AND TEXTURE DIMENSIONS THAT SATISFY THE PALATE IN MORE HEALTHFUL WAYS THAN HEAVY DRESSINGS. SEMI-SWEET PAPAYA COMBINES WONDERFULLY WITH THE SALTY BLUE CHEESE, ORIENTAL VINAIGRETTE, AND MIXED BABY GREENS IN THIS RECIPE. IT ALSO PROVIDES SPECIFIC ENZYMES THAT AID IN DIGESTION.

Salmon

1/2 cup soy sauce
3 tablespoons toasted sesame oil
6 (6 ounces each) boneless skinless salmon fillets
1/2 teaspoon salt
1/4 teaspoon ground black pepper
2/3 cup sesame seeds (about 3 ounces)
4 tablespoons vegetable or canola oil

Oriental Vinaigrette

1/4 cup rice vinegar
2 tablespoons peanut butter (optional)
2 tablespoons soy sauce
1 tablespoon Dijon mustard
1 tablespoon grated fresh ginger
1 tablespoon honey
1 tablespoon minced shallots
1/2 teaspoon ground black pepper
1/2 teaspoon salt
1/4 cup toasted sesame oil
1/2 cup vegetable oil
1/3 cup crumbled blue cheese

Salad

8 ounces mixed baby greens
  Salt and ground black pepper, to taste
1 ripe papaya, peeled, seeded, and diced
1/3 cup crumbled blue cheese

To make the salmon: Preheat the oven to 350°F. Mix the soy sauce and sesame oil in a medium bowl. Sprinkle the salmon with salt and pepper. Place the sesame seeds in a pie dish or baking dish. Working with 1 fillet at a time, dip the fillets in the soy sauce mixture, then coat the tops and bottoms of the fillets in the sesame seeds (do not coat the sides with the sesame seeds).

Heat 2 tablespoons of oil on a heavy large griddle over medium heat. Place 3 salmon fillets on the griddle and cook just until the sesame crust is golden brown, about 4 minutes per side (the salmon will not be cooked through at this point). Using a metal spatula, transfer the fillets to a heavy large rimmed baking sheet. Wipe off the griddle and repeat with the remaining vegetable oil and salmon fillets. Bake until the salmon fillets are just cooked through, about 5 minutes. Cool the salmon fillets completely, then cover, and refrigerate.

Meanwhile prepare the oriental vinaigrette: Blend the vinegar, peanut butter, soy sauce, mustard, ginger, honey, shallots, salt, and black pepper in a blender until smooth. With the machine running, gradually blend in the sesame oil, then the vegetable oil.

To assemble the salad: Toss the mixed greens in a large bowl with enough vinaigrette to coat. Season the salad to taste with salt and pepper. Mound the salad atop each of 6 plates. Sprinkle the papaya and blue cheese over the salad. Top with the chilled salmon fillets, and serve.

COOK'S NOTES: Papayas should be tender enough to cut through easily when you serve them. If you purchase papayas that are hard, put them in a brown paper bag in your cupboard. They will ripen within a few days. If papaya isn't your thing, substitute diced mango or cantaloupe.

The sesame-crusted salmon, served hot or cold, and oriental vinaigrette will taste delightful on an array of salads. Try them with a salad of baby spinach and thinly sliced red onions, or a salad of shredded carrots, thinly sliced Napa cabbage and red cabbage.

The salmon and vinaigrette can be made 1 day ahead. Cover them separately and refrigerate. Rewhisk the vinaigrette before tossing it with the mixed baby greens.

Serves 6

GRILLED SWORDFISH WITH TOMATOES, OLIVES, AND OREGANO

THE ANCHOVIES AND SERRANO CHILIES ADD A REAL ZIP TO THIS CLASSIC MEDITERRANEAN DISH. IT'S ABSOLUTELY FABULOUS SERVED WITH A SIDE OF CLASSIC RICE PILAF (PAGE 133) OR ATOP A MOUND OF FRESH FETTUCCINE. GRILLED BOK CHOY, BRAISED SPINACH OR SWISS CHARD WITH GARLIC ALSO MAKE GOOD ACCOMPANIMENTS.

4 tablespoons olive oil
8 ounces fresh mushrooms (such as oyster, cremini, white button, or stemmed shiitake), sliced
1 tablespoon minced garlic
4 large plum tomatoes, chopped
3/4 cup pitted Kalamata olives, halved
1/4 cup finely chopped cilantro leaves
3 tablespoons fresh lemon juice
2 tablespoons finely chopped fresh Italian parsley
2 tablespoons finely chopped fresh oregano
3 anchovy fillets, minced
1 tablespoon drained capers
1 tablespoon minced serrano chilies
1 teaspoon ground black pepper
1 teaspoon salt
6 (6- to 7-ounces each and 1-inch-thick)
   swordfish fillets
   Oregano sprigs, for garnish

Prepare the barbecue for medium-high heat. Heat 2 tablespoons of oil in a heavy large skillet over medium-high heat. Add the mushrooms and garlic and sauté until the garlic is golden, about 2 minutes. Add the tomatoes, olives, cilantro, lemon juice, parsley, oregano, anchovies, capers, chilies, and 1/2 teaspoon each of black pepper and salt. Sauté until the mixture is heated through but the tomatoes still hold their shape, about 2 minutes. Remove from the heat and cover to keep the mushroom-tomato mixture warm while grilling the fish.

Rub the remaining 2 tablespoons of oil over the fish, then sprinkle with the remaining 1/2 teaspoon each of salt and black pepper. Grill the fish until it is just cooked through, about 3 minutes per side.

Transfer the fish to plates. Spoon the mushroom-tomato mixture atop the fish. Garnish with oregano sprigs and serve.

COOK'S NOTES: The olives, anchovies, and capers lend salt to the sauce, don't season the sauce with more salt until it has finished cooking.

Serves 6

SIMPLE POACHED SALMON

THIS METHOD OF POACHING IS ONE OF THE EASIEST AND FOOLPROOF WAYS TO PREPARE SALMON. IT'S REALLY AS EASY AS BRINGING THE POACHING LIQUID TO A SIMMER, THEN TURNING OFF THE HEAT, AND LETTING THE SALMON COOK IN THE LIQUID. SINCE THE FISH COOKS GENTLY IN A VERY DELICATE ENVIRONMENT, IT BECOMES MOIST AND SUCCULENT. AND BECAUSE IT'S SO EASY TO PREPARE, THIS DISH MAKES A FABULOUS BUFFET ITEM FOR LARGE PARTIES. TAHINI SAUCE (PAGE 34) IS A GREAT MATCH WITH THIS SALMON, AND WHEN SERVED WITH ORZO SALAD WITH SUN-DRIED TOMATOES AND KALAMATA OLIVES (PAGE 60) IT'S A TERRIFIC PICNIC MEAL. FOR THOSE OF US SHORT ON TIME, IT'S ALSO PERFECT FOR QUICK DINNERS.

6 cups water
1 cup dry white wine
1/4 cup white distilled vinegar
2 large onions, thinly sliced
3 carrots, peeled and thinly sliced
3 celery stalks, thinly sliced
2 bay leaves
2 tablespoons fresh thyme leaves
6 whole black peppercorns
2 teaspoons salt
1/2 teaspoon coarsely ground black pepper (page 18)
6 (6-ounces each) boneless skinless salmon fillets

Place the water in a heavy 12-inch-diameter skillet with 2-inch-high sides. Cover and bring the water to a boil over high heat. Stir in the wine and vinegar. Add the onions, carrots, celery, bay leaves, thyme, and whole peppercorns. Cover and bring to a boil. Decrease the heat to medium and simmer until the onions are translucent and the liquid is flavorful, about 45 minutes. Strain the broth and discard the solids. Return the broth to the same skillet.

Sprinkle the salmon with the salt and coarsely ground pepper. Submerge the salmon fillets in the broth (the salmon should be completely submerged in the broth). Bring the broth to a simmer over medium-high heat. Remove from the heat. Cover and let stand until the salmon is just cooked through, about 20 minutes.

Using a long metal spatula, transfer the salmon fillets to plates and serve immediately.

COOK'S NOTES: Poaching is a technique whereby the food item is completely submerged in a liquid that is kept at a constant moderate temperature, so be sure to completely submerge the fillets. For easy removal, try not to crowd the fillets in the skillet. If you are unable to find a large skillet, you can also use a roasting pan with 2-inch high sides.

If you are serving the salmon fillets cold, keep them in the broth until they have cooled. Cover and refrigerate until ready to serve. This method keeps the salmon moist and tender. The salmon will keep for 3 to 4 days in the broth, covered and refrigerated. The poaching liquid can be frozen for 2 weeks and used as a fish stock.

Serves 6

DESSERT

AND BREADS

This chapter represents my favorite desserts. They include dried fruits, puddings, pistachio-stuffed pastries bathed in syrup, and other sweets. The recipes demonstrate that many bakery-scrumptious desserts are possible to make easily at home.

VIETNAM 2000

Though I had been eating and cooking rice for decades, only recently did I come to perceive it as more than a staple. My daughter and I participated in a culinary tour of Vietnam, bussed from city to village, sampling local cuisine and cooking methods. Each leg of our journey offered the same view—green strips of fields to the horizon edged by bushy trees. Shimmering lines of water separated the fields into clean rectangles. Women, bent by the heat and wearing button-like traditional hats, were weaving through the rows, working the stalk-filled paddies.

Our bus stopped along the road so we could get a better look at the rice still clinging to its stalks. As we stepped out of the bus, the thick Vietnamese air enveloped us, but the warm smiles of the women in the fields lessened the air's oppressiveness. They stopped their work to greet us enthusiastically, then started again as we watched. Some of the women heaved large bundles of rice onto their shoulders and beat them against a tall grate. This jarred showers of rice kernels from the stalk, which fell into large barrels in impressive amounts. Their labor, weighted by the tropical heat, seemed incredibly difficult, and the women's bright dispositions amazed me. Only the aroma of the rice—sweet, humble jasmine—helped explain their ease; the entire landscape breathed its sweetness.

This sweetness also can also be found in my popular rice pudding, which is easy to prepare and a favorite of dessert lovers. Its sweet flavor is achieved using vanilla beans instead of vanilla extract -- a healthier alternative. In our recipe, the vanilla flavor is more natural, the texture more earthy. Our rice pudding has no egg. This doesn't compromise flavor. Instead, it allows the innate sweetness of the rice to emerge. The raspberry purée compliments its subtle sweetness, and a hint of crunchy nuts jazz it up a bit. The result is a light, completely satisfying dessert, always a crowd-pleaser at Zov's Bistro.

JASMINE RICE PUDDING WITH FRESH BERRIES

THE CRUNCHINESS OF THE PISTACHIO AND THE TARTNESS OF FRESH BERRIES COMBINED WITH THE SWEET FRAGRANCE OF JASMINE RICE MAKE THIS A MAGICAL DESSERT. SERVE IT IN PRETTY INDIVIDUAL BOWLS OR IN A LARGE DECORATIVE GLASS BOWL.

2 cups water
1 cup uncooked jasmine rice
4 cups whole or lowfat milk
2 cups whipping cream
3/4 cup sugar
1 vanilla bean, split lengthwise
2 cups assorted fresh berries (such as raspberries,
  blueberries, blackberries, and sliced strawberries)
1/2 cup shelled raw pistachios, coarsely chopped

Combine water and the rice in a heavy large pot. Bring the water to a boil over medium-high heat. Decrease the heat to low. Cover and simmer until the rice is tender and the water is absorbed, about 12 minutes. Stir in the milk, cream, and sugar. Scrape the seeds from the vanilla bean into the rice mixture and add the bean to the rice mixture. Bring to a simmer over medium-high heat. Decrease the heat to medium-low and continue cooking until the mixture thickens slightly (the consistency will look like cooked oatmeal when done, and will continue to thicken as it cools), stirring often, about 35 minutes. Remove the vanilla bean.

Pour the hot pudding into a large bowl and immediately cover it with plastic wrap to prevent a skin from forming on top. Refrigerate until the pudding is cold, at least 6 hours and up to 1 day.

Spoon the pudding into individual glass bowls. Spoon the berries atop the pudding. Sprinkle the pistachios over and serve.

COOK'S NOTES: You can buy jasmine rice at Asian grocery stores, natural foods stores, and some supermarkets. If jasmine rice is not available, use a medium-grain white rice, such as arborio rice, instead.

One teaspoon of vanilla extract may be used in place of the vanilla bean, if desired. As an alternative to the fresh berries, drizzle raspberry puree over the pudding just before serving.

Be sure not to cook the pudding until it is very thick, since it will continue to thicken as it cools.

Serves 6 to 8

CARAMELIZED APPLES WITH COGNAC AND VANILLA ICE CREAM

THIS DESSERT IS FOR ALL APPLE LOVERS. THE COMBINATION OF APPLES AND COGNAC IS REALLY AMAZING. THE KEY IS TO SERVE THE APPLES WARM. ADD A SCOOP OF VANILLA ICE CREAM AND YOU'LL THINK YOU'VE DIED AND GONE TO HEAVEN!

1/2 cup (1 stick) unsalted butter
2 3/4 pounds Granny Smith apples (about 7),
*   peeled, cored, and cut into 1/4-inch-thick slices*
1/2 cup sugar
1/2 teaspoon ground cinnamon
2 tablespoons cognac
1 pint vanilla ice cream
*   Fresh raspberries, for garnish*
*   Mint sprigs, for garnish*

Melt the butter in a heavy large frying pan over high heat, stirring until the butter foams and becomes golden, about 2 minutes. Toss the apples, sugar, and cinnamon in a large bowl to coat. Immediately add the apple mixture to the hot butter. Stir the apples to coat with the butter. Simmer until the juices evaporate and the apples become caramelized, stirring occasionally, about 12 minutes. Using a slotted spoon, transfer the caramelized apples back to the large bowl. Discard any remaining butter in the pan. Stir the cognac into the caramelized apples.

Spoon the warm caramelized apples into bowls. Top with a scoop of ice cream. Garnish with fresh raspberries and mint sprigs. Serve immediately.

COOK'S NOTES: As the apples cook, they will release their juices. Be sure to allow time for these juices to form and evaporate. Once the juices evaporate, the apples will then caramelize.

If desired, stir 1/4 cup of golden raisins and 1/4 cup of chopped toasted walnuts, pecans, or almonds into the caramelized apples.

Try layering the caramelized apples between sheets of baked puffed pastry or phyllo dough for a delicious apple napoleon. They are also fabulous as a topping for pancakes and waffles.

Serves 4 to 6

ROSEMARY-PARMESAN SCONES

TENDER, DELECTABLE AND SCRUMPTIOUS! THESE HERBED SCONES COMPLIMENT SO MANY MEALS, OR TRY THEM ON THEIR OWN, FOR AN AFTERNOON TEA. YOU CAN EVEN FORM THE SCONES ONE DAY BEFORE SERVING, CHILL, THEN BAKE FOR LUNCH OR DINNER THE NEXT DAY.

3 cups all purpose flour
2 tablespoons sugar
2 1/2 teaspoons baking powder
3/4 teaspoon salt
1/2 teaspoon baking soda
1 1/2 sticks (3/4 cup) unsalted butter,
  chilled and cut into small pieces
1 cup (or more) buttermilk
1/2 cup plus 2 tablespoons freshly grated
  Parmesan cheese
2 tablespoons chopped fresh rosemary
1 tablespoon unsalted butter, melted

Preheat the oven to 400°F. Line a heavy large baking sheet with parchment paper. Stir the flour, sugar, baking powder, salt, and baking soda in a medium bowl to blend. Add the chilled butter pieces. Using your fingertips or a pastry blender, cut the butter into the dry ingredients until the mixture resembles a coarse cornmeal. Add the buttermilk, 1/2 cup of Parmesan cheese, and the rosemary. Stir until the ingredients are just moistened and a soft, rough dough forms, adding more buttermilk 1 tablespoon at a time if the mixture is too dry. Gather the dough into a ball. Transfer it to a lightly floured work surface and knead just until it holds together.

Roll out the dough to a 9-inch-diameter disc that is about 1/2 to 3/4-inch thick. Using a 2 1/2- to 3-inch-diameter biscuit cutter, cut the dough into circles. Place the scones on the prepared baking sheet. Gather the scraps, then reroll and cut out more scones. Brush the dough with the melted butter, then sprinkle with the remaining 2 tablespoons of Parmesan cheese. Bake until the scones puff and the tops and bottoms are golden, about 18 minutes. Transfer the scones to a rack to cool slightly.

COOK'S NOTES: Unbaked scones will keep for one week in the freezer. Thaw the scones on a baking sheet lined with parchment paper, then bake them in a 400°F oven until they puff and become golden. They're best served warm, but are still delicious at room temperature.

For a variation, add 2 tablespoons of lemon zest and substitute the rosemary with chopped fresh thyme. For a terrific breakfast scone, just omit the Parmesan cheese and rosemary altogether, and add 1/2 cup of sugar, 2 tablespoons of orange zest, and 1 tablespoon of lavender. Adding currants or dried cranberries, make another terrific variation. They are even delicious plain.

Makes 12

CRÈME CARAMEL

EVERY HOLIDAY, MY SISTER-IN-LAW ANOUSH NEED NOT ASK WHAT TO BRING. IT'S A GIVEN. NO HOLIDAY IS COMPLETE WITHOUT HER WONDERFUL CRÈME CARAMEL. THIS CHILLED, FLAN-LIKE DESSERT IS SILKY SMOOTH. AND, BECAUSE IT'S MADE WITH MILK INSTEAD OF CREAM AND WHOLE EGGS INSTEAD OF EGG YOLKS, IT IS MUCH LIGHTER THAN CRÈME BRÛLÉE (LESS GUILT!).

Caramel
1 1/2 cups sugar
1/3 cup water

Custard
5 cups whole milk
1 1/2 cups sugar
1 teaspoon grated lemon peel
1 teaspoon grated orange peel
1 vanilla bean, split lengthwise
8 large eggs
  Assorted fresh berries or
  other seasonal fruit, for garnish

To make the caramel: Stir the sugar and water in a heavy medium saucepan over low heat until the sugar dissolves. Increase the heat to medium-high and boil the syrup without stirring, until it turns a deep amber color, swirling the pan occasionally, about 12 minutes. As the syrup cooks, wipe down the sides of the pan with a wet pastry brush to remove any sugar crystals. Immediately pour the caramel into a 10-inch-diameter cake pan with 2-inch-high sides. Using oven mitts (the pan will get really hot!), quickly rotate the pan to coat the sides with the caramel. Place the pan in a large roasting pan. Set aside to cool.

To make the custard: Position the rack in the center of the oven and preheat the oven to 350°F. Combine the milk, sugar, lemon peel, and orange peel in a large saucepan. Scrape the seeds from the vanilla bean into the milk mixture, then add the vanilla bean.

Bring to a simmer over medium heat, whisking until the sugar is dissolved. Remove from the heat. Cover and let stand for 10 minutes.

Whisk the eggs in a large bowl to blend. Gradually whisk in the warm milk mixture. Strain the custard through a fine-meshed strainer and into an 8-cup measuring cup; discarding the solids. Pour the custard over the caramel in the pan. Carefully pour enough hot water into the roasting pan (around the cake pan) to reach halfway up the sides of the cake pan. Bake until the custard is just set around the edges but still wobbles in the center when the pan is gently shaken, about 1 hour and 15 minutes.

Transfer the cake pan to a cooling rack and cool for 30 minutes. Loosely cover the cake pan with plastic wrap and refrigerate overnight (the custard will become set in the center as it is cools. Refrigerating the custard overnight also allows enough time for the hardened caramel to dissolve into a sauce).

Run a small sharp knife around the pan sides to help loosen the custard from the pan. Place a cake platter with a 1-inch rim atop the custard. Holding the platter and cake pan together, invert the custard onto the platter, shaking the custard gently, if necessary, to release it onto the platter. Scrape up any caramel from the bottom of the pan and spoon it over the custard. Garnish with fresh berries or other seasonal fruit and serve.

COOK'S NOTES: It is important to cook the caramel just until it becomes a golden syrup. If it becomes too dark it develops a burnt flavor. Cooling the milk mixture slightly before stirring it into the eggs helps prevent the eggs from curdling.

If vanilla beans are not available, add 1 teaspoon of vanilla extract to the cooled milk mixture instead.

For individual crème caramels, distribute the caramel among 6-ounce soufflé dishes or custard cups and decrease the baking time to about 45 minutes.

Serve 8 to 10

KATAIFI WITH RICOTTA CUSTARD AND ORANGE BLOSSOM SYRUP

WHEN YOU ARE IN THE MOOD TO INDULGE, THIS IS THE RECIPE FOR YOU!! THIS DESSERT IS SENSATIONAL. OFFER IT WARM FOR DESSERT WITH A CUP OF TEA, OR SERVE IT AS A SWEET TREAT FOR BRUNCH OR ANYTIME OF THE DAY.

Syrup

2 cups sugar

2 cups water

1 teaspoon fresh lemon juice

2 tablespoons orange blossom water

Pastry

8 ounces (half of 16-ounce package) kataifi
  (shredded phyllo dough), thawed if frozen

1/2 cup (1 stick) unsalted butter, melted

2 cups heavy whipping cream

1 cup sugar

2 cups half and half

3/4 cup cornstarch

1 pound ricotta cheese

3 tablespoons orange blossom water

To make the syrup: Stir the sugar, water, and lemon juice in a heavy medium saucepan to blend. Bring the mixture to a boil over high heat. Continue boiling for 3 minutes. As the syrup cooks, wipe down the sides of the pan with a wet pastry brush to remove any sugar crystals. Remove from the heat and stir in the orange blossom water. Set aside to cool.

Meanwhile, make the pastry: Preheat the oven to 375°F. Pull apart the strands of kataifi to separate them. Using a large sharp knife, very coarsely chop the strands. Toss the kataifi with the melted butter in a large bowl to coat completely. Arrange half of the kataifi over the bottom of a 13x9x2-inch baking dish, covering completely. Set the remaining kataifi aside.

Stir the cream, sugar, and 1 cup of half and half in a heavy large saucepan to blend. Whisk the remaining 1 cup of half and half and the cornstarch in a medium bowl until smooth. Bring the cream mixture in the saucepan to a boil. Whisk in the ricotta cheese, then whisk in the cornstarch mixture. Continue whisking until the custard comes to a simmer and becomes thick, about 2 minutes. Pour the hot custard over the kataifi in the baking dish, spreading to cover completely and evenly. Sprinkle the remaining kataifi evenly over the custard.

Bake until the kataifi is golden brown, about 45 minutes to 1 hour. Set aside to cool slightly. Using a large sharp knife cut the pastry into 12 pieces. Using a metal spatula, transfer the pastry to plates. Drizzle 3 to 4 tablespoons of syrup over each and serve immediately.

COOK'S NOTES: Kataifi is finely shredded phyllo dough that is available in the frozen or refrigerated foods section of Middle Eastern or Greek markets. Orange blossom water can be found at Indian or Persian markets, natural health foods stores, specialty stores, and some supermarkets. If it's not available, use Grand Marnier instead.

Chopped pistachios or candied orange peel make terrific garnishes to this fabulous dessert, and orange segments pair beautifully with it.

Serves 12 to 16

APRICOT COFFEE CAKE

THIS IS A DELIGHTFUL, EASY, AND FUN CAKE TO MAKE. THE APRICOT PRESERVES AND LATTICE TOPPING MAKE IT A PRETTY CAKE TO TAKE ALONG TO A POTLUCK OR TO SERVE WITH AFTERNOON TEA.

Nonstick vegetable oil cooking spray
3 cups all purpose flour
2 teaspoons baking powder
1/2 teaspoon salt
1 1/2 cups sugar
1 cup solid vegetable shortening
8 large egg yolks
1 teaspoon vanilla extract
1 cup sour cream
1 cup apricot preserves
Powdered sugar, for sifting

Preheat the oven to 350°F. Spray a 9-inch square cake pan with nonstick spray. Line the pan with parchment paper, allowing the paper to hang over 2 sides of the pan (this will make it easy to lift the cake out of the pan). Spray the paper with nonstick spray.

Whisk the flour, baking powder, and salt in a medium bowl to blend. Using an electric mixer, beat the sugar and shortening in a large bowl until fluffy. Add the egg yolks 1 at a time, beating until well blended before each addition. Beat in the vanilla. Add the flour mixture in 3 additions, alternating with the sour cream in 2 additions.

Spread two-thirds of the batter over the prepared pan. Spread the apricot preserves evenly over the batter. Transfer the remaining batter to a piping bag that is fitted with a large star tip. Pipe the batter atop the apricot preserves to form a lattice pattern.

Bake until the lattice is golden brown and a tester inserted into the center of the cake comes out with no cake batter attached (the preserves may be attached to the tester), about 1 hour. Cool the cake to room temperature.

When ready to serve, run a knife around the cake to loosen it from the pan. Using the parchment paper overhang, lift the cake out of the pan. Cut the cake into 16 squares, and arrange on a platter. Sift powdered sugar over the cake squares and serve.

COOK'S NOTES: Raspberry or strawberry jam can be substituted for the apricot preserves. This cake can be made 1 day ahead and stored in an airtight container at room temperature.

Serves 16

CARAMEL NUT POPCORN

IF YOU LOVE CARAMEL CORN YOU'RE IN FOR A REAL TREAT! LOADED WITH PECANS AND ALMONDS AND COATED IN A BUTTERY CARAMEL, THIS EASY CARAMEL POPCORN MAKES AN ADDICTIVE SNACK AND A WONDERFUL GIFT, IF YOU'RE WILLING TO PART WITH IT.

8 cups freshly popped popcorn
   (from about 1/3 cup kernels)
1 1/3 cups pecan halves, toasted
2/3 cup sliced almonds, toasted
   Nonstick vegetable oil cooking spray
1 cup (2 sticks) unsalted butter
1 1/2 cups granulatedsugar
1/2 cup light corn syrup
2 teaspoons vanilla extract
1/8 teaspoon salt

Toss the popcorn, pecans, and almonds in a large bowl and set aside.

Spray a large baking sheet with nonstick spray. Melt the butter in a heavy medium saucepan over medium-high heat. Whisk in the sugar and corn syrup. Bring the mixture to a boil, whisking constantly. Boil until the caramel sauce is pale golden and a candy thermometer inserted into the caramel sauce registers 300°F, stirring often, about 6 minutes. Remove the pan from the heat. Whisk in the vanilla and salt. Immediately pour the caramel sauce over the popcorn and nuts. Using two large oiled wooden spoons, toss the popcorn and nuts to coat with the caramel sauce. Transfer the caramel corn to the prepared baking sheet, spreading in an even layer. Set aside to cool completely (the caramel will harden as the mixture cools). Break the caramel corn into desired pieces.

COOK'S NOTES: The caramel popcorn can be made 1 week ahead. Store it in an airtight container at room temperature.

You'll need a candy thermometer to make sure the caramel sauce reaches the "hard-ball" stage (300°F). It's at this stage that the sauce will harden once cool.

Makes about 1 3/4 pounds (12 cups)

KHATA WITH STREUSEL (ARMENIAN TEA-CAKE)

THE STREUSEL FILLING IN THIS DELIGHTFUL OLD ARMENIAN RECIPE IS WHAT MAKES IT UNFORGETTABLE. YOU CAN PREPARE THE TEA-CAKE A WEEK AHEAD OF TIME AND KEEP IT BAKED IN THE FREEZER, OR YOU CAN FREEZE IT UNBAKED, TIGHTLY SEALED, AND BAKE LATER FOR FRESHNESS. IT IS FANTASTIC WITH AFTERNOON TEA OR, AS I LOVE TO ENJOY IT, FIRST THING IN THE MORNING WITH COFFEE.

Streusel Filling

1/2 cup (1 stick) unsalted butter, room temperature
1 1/2 cups sugar
1 1/4 cups all purpose flour
  Pinch of salt

Dough

3/4 cup warm water (105°F to 115°F)
2 (1/4 ounce) envelopes dry yeast (4 teaspoons)
3/4 cup evaporated milk
1/2 cup vegetable oil
3 large eggs
1 teaspoon salt
5 1/4 cups all purpose flour, plus more for dusting
3/4 cup (1 1/2 sticks) unsalted butter, melted
1 beaten egg mixed with 1 tablespoon of water, for glaze

To make the filling: Using an electric mixer beat the butter in a large bowl until pale and fluffy. Beat in the sugar. Add the flour and beat just until blended (the mixture will have a loose sandy texture). Cover and refrigerate.

To make the dough: Using a heavy-duty stand mixer fitted with the paddle attachment, mix the warm water and yeast in a large bowl to blend. Let stand until the yeast dissolves. Mix in the milk, oil, eggs, and salt. Gradually mix in 5 1/4 cups of flour (the dough will look wet). Replace the paddle attachment with the dough hook and knead until the dough is smooth and elastic, about 2 minutes. Or, to knead by hand, transfer the dough to a floured work surface and knead until it is smooth and elastic, about 3 minutes. Divide the dough into 6 equal pieces. Shape the dough pieces into balls. Arrange the dough balls on a lightly floured baking sheet. Cover with plastic wrap, and a clean kitchen towel and let the dough balls rise in a warm draft-free area until they double in volume, about 1 hour.

Roll out 1 dough ball on a floured work surface to a 14x12-inch rectangle. Brush away any excess flour from atop the dough. Brush some melted butter over the dough. Fold one-third of the dough over the center third. Brush away any excess flour from the folded side. Fold the remaining third over the folded two-thirds as is done for a letter. Brush away any excess flour from atop the folded dough, then brush with butter. Fold the opposite ends in to meet at the center of the folded dough. Brush away any excess flour from atop the folded dough, then brush the top with butter (the folded dough will be a smaller rectangle at this point). Fold the top and bottom sides of the dough in to meet at the center again. Fold to close, as for a book. Place the folded dough seam side down on a baking sheet and cover with plastic wrap. Repeat with the remaining 5 dough balls. Refrigerate until cold, about 1 hour.

To form the rolls: Line 2 heavy, large baking sheets with parchment paper. Roll out 1 folded piece of dough on a lightly floured work surface to an 11x9-inch rectangle. Spoon 2/3 cup of the filling over the dough, patting down to adhere and leaving a 1/2-inch border along 1 long side. Starting at the other long side, roll up the dough in a cinnamon-roll style, forming a log. Moisten the edge with water, then pinch the seam to seal. Using unwaxed dental floss, cut the log crosswise into 6 equal pieces. Arrange the rolls seam side down on the prepared baking sheet. Cover with plastic wrap, then a kitchen towel. Repeat with remaining folded dough pieces and filling. Pat the rolls to flatten slightly. (The rolls can be made up to this point 1 week ahead. Store them in an airtight container and freeze. Thaw the rolls before continuing). Let the rolls rise in a warm draft-free area until doubled in volume, about 1 hour. Meanwhile, preheat the oven to 350°F.

Bake the rolls until the tops are golden brown, about 25 minutes. Cool slightly. Serve the rolls warm.

LUSCIOUS LEMON SQUARES

THESE SQUARES FEATURE A BEAUTIFULLY SIMPLE YET RICH SHORTBREAD COOKIE CRUST. THE TENDER CRUMBS OFFER THE PERFECT LEVEL OF SWEETNESS TO ACCOMPANY THE SLIGHT BITE OF THE LEMON CURD. CUT INTO SMALL SQUARES, THEY LOOK LIKE LITTLE CANDIES, JUST WAITING TO BE SAVORED.

To make the crust: Preheat the oven to 350°F. Spray an 8-inch square baking dish with nonstick spray. Blend the butter, powdered sugar, and salt in a food processor until moist crumbs form. Add the flour. Using the on off button, pulse just until the flour is incorporated and moist crumbs form. Gently press the dough evenly over the bottom of the prepared dish (not the sides). Bake until the crust is pale golden on top, about 30 minutes.

Meanwhile, to prepare the lemon topping: Whisk the granulated sugar, eggs, flour, lemon peel, and salt in a large bowl to blend. Whisk in the lemon juice. Pour the lemon mixture over the hot baked crust. Bake until the lemon mixture is just set in the center, about 20 minutes. Transfer to a cooling rack and cool completely. Cover and refrigerate until cold.

Cut the pastry into 16 squares. Dust the lemon squares with powdered sugar, and serve.

COOK'S NOTES: Try substituting the lemon juice and lemon zest with lime juice and lime zest.

Crust
  Nonstick vegetable oil cooking spray
1/2 cup (1 stick) cold unsalted butter,
  cut into 1-inch pieces
1/2 cup powdered sugar
  Pinch of salt
1 cup all purpose flour

Lemon Topping
1 cup granulated sugar
6 large eggs
2 tablespoons all purpose flour
2 tablespoons grated lemon peel
  Pinch of salt
3/4 cup fresh lemon juice
  Powdered sugar, for dusting

MANGO-LIME PARFAITS

THIS ELEGANT, REFRESHING PARFAIT IS EASY TO PREPARE AND JUST PERFECT FOR SUMMER AFTERNOON ENTERTAINING. TRY SUBSTITUTING PAPAYA IF MANGOES ARE NOT AVAILABLE, AND SERVE EACH PARFAIT WITH A SIMPLE SHORTBREAD COOKIE. YOUR GUESTS WILL BE SO IMPRESSED!

6 firm ripe large mangoes, peeled and pitted
4 tablespoons sugar
2 tablespoons fresh lime juice
1 teaspoon grated lime peel
3/4 cup heavy whipping cream
1/4 cup sliced almonds, toasted
8 mint sprigs, for garnish

Blend 2 mangoes with 2 tablespoons of sugar in a food processor until smooth. Strain the mango puree through a meshed strainer and into a medium bowl; discard the fibrous solids in the strainer. Stir the lime juice and lime peel into the mango puree.

Cut the remaining 4 mangoes into 1/4- to 1/2-inch pieces. Stir one-fourth (about 1 cup) of the mango pieces into the mango puree. Cover and refrigerate the puree and remaining mango pieces separately until cold, at least 3 hours.

Using an electric mixer, beat the cream with the remaining 2 tablespoons of sugar in a large bowl until soft peaks form. Fold the mango puree into the whipped cream.

Layer the mango puree and reserved mango pieces decoratively in 8 parfait glasses. Sprinkle with the almonds. Garnish with the mint sprigs and serve.

COOK'S NOTES: There are lots of possible variations for these easy and delicious parfaits. For instance, the mangoes can be substituted with ripe peaches, berries, or any of your favorite summer fruit. Orange juice and orange zest can be used instead of the lime juice and zest. And if desired, crushed amaretti cookies or biscotti can be sprinkled over the parfaits instead of the almonds.

The parfaits can be assembled and refrigerated up to 8 hours before serving.

Serves 8

SESAME SEED RING ROLLS

THESE ARE THE MOST POPULAR DINNER ROLLS AMONG MY FAMILY. THEY ARE MADE OF A SIMPLE YEAST DOUGH THAT YOU CAN JUST KNEAD, ROLL AND BAKE. THE SESAME SEEDS LEND A WONDERFULLY NUTTY FLAVOR. THESE ROLLS CAN BE FROZEN AFTER THEY HAVE BEEN BAKED.

3 cups warm water (105°F to 115°F)
4 tablespoons sugar
2 (1/4-ounce) envelopes dry yeast (4 teaspoons)
8 1/2 cups all purpose flour
2 teaspoon salt
1/4 cup plus 1 teaspoon olive oil
1 1/2 cups sesame seeds (8 ounces)
3 tablespoons whole milk

Stir 1/2 cup of warm water, 1 tablespoon of sugar, and the yeast in a small bowl to blend. Set aside until the yeast dissolves and the mixture is foamy, about 10 minutes.

Using a heavy-duty stand mixer with the hook attachment, stir the flour, salt, and remaining 3 tablespoons of sugar in a large bowl to blend. Mix in 1/4 cup of oil. Stir in the yeast mixture. Gradually stir in enough of the remaining 2 1/2 cups of water to form a soft dough. Transfer the dough to a floured work surface and knead until smooth and elastic, about 2 minutes. Form the dough into a ball.

Using 1 teaspoon of oil, lightly oil the clean mixing bowl. Return the dough to the bowl and turn to coat with the oil. Cover with plastic and let stand in a warm draft-free area until doubled in volume, about 1 hour.

Stir the sesame seeds and milk in a pie plate to coat. Set the sesame seed mixture aside. Lightly oil 2 heavy large baking sheets. Punch down the dough. Turn the dough out onto a floured work surface. Divide the dough equally into 16 pieces. Working with 1 piece of dough at a time, roll the dough between the palm of your hand and the work surface into a ball. Arrange the dough balls on the prepared baking sheets, spacing evenly apart. Dust the tops with flour. Cover with plastic wrap.

Preheat the oven to 400°F. Lightly oil 2 more heavy large baking sheets (you will need 4 baking sheets total). Using a floured 1 1/2-inch-diameter biscuit cutter, cut out a hole in the center of each roll (the rolls will resemble doughnuts). Dip each doughnut-shaped roll into the sesame seed mixture to coat completely. If necessary, gently stretch the rolls so that they are 3 inches in diameter. Arrange 4 rolls on each baking sheet. Cover with plastic and let rise again in a draft-free area for 45 minutes.

Working in batches, bake the rolls until they puff and are very pale golden, about 10 minutes. Cool slightly on the baking sheets. Serve warm.

COOK'S NOTES: The rolls can be made 1 day ahead. Store in an airtight container or resealable plastic bag. Wrap the rolls in foil and warm in the oven before serving.

Makes 16 rolls

BREAD PUDDING WITH CHOCOLATE CHUNKS AND BANANAS

BANANA AND CHOCOLATE ARE A MARRIAGE MADE IN HEAVEN. CREATED BY MICHELLE BRACKEN, A LONG TIME PASTRY CHEF AT THE RESTAURANT, IT'S NO WONDER THAT THIS DELICIOUS BREAD PUDDING WITH LARGE CHUNKS OF OOZING MELTED CHOCOLATE INTERMINGLED AMIDST RICH BRIOCHE BREAD PUDDING AND CREAMY VANILLA SAUCE HAS BECOME ONE OF OUR MOST POPULAR DESSERTS.

3 tablespoons unsalted butter
3 medium bananas, peeled and cut into
  1/2-inch-thick slices
2 cups heavy whipping cream
2 cups whole milk
1 cup sugar
8 large eggs
1 tablespoon vanilla extract
8 ounces coarsely chopped bittersweet chocolate
1 pound day-old brioche or challah bread,
  cut into 1/2-inch cubes
Vanilla Sauce (recipe follows)
Powdered sugar, for dusting

Preheat the oven to 350°F. Coat a 13x9x2-inch baking dish with 1 tablespoon of butter. Melt the remaining 2 tablespoons of butter in a heavy small skillet over medium-high heat until it foams, about 1 minute. Add the banana and toss to coat. Using a fork, very coarsely mash the bananas. Set aside to cool.

Whisk the cream, milk, sugar, eggs, and vanilla in a large bowl to blend. Fold in the mashed bananas and chopped chocolate. Add the bread cubes and toss to coat. Let the mixture stand for 25 minutes, tossing occasionally, to allow the bread to absorb the custard. Transfer the mixture to the prepared baking dish, spreading evenly.

Bake until the center is set and the bread pudding is golden brown on top, about 55 minutes. Let stand 30 minutes to cool slightly.

Cut the warm bread pudding into squares. Transfer the bread pudding to plates and spoon the cold Vanilla Sauce around the bread pudding. Dust with powdered sugar and serve.

COOK'S NOTES: As a phenomenal alternative, serve this bread pudding with good-quality chocolate or vanilla ice cream instead of the Vanilla Sauce. For another variation, add 1/4 cup of coffee liqueur to the custard.

Although bittersweet chocolate works best in this bread pudding, semisweet chocolate chips may be used as a quick substitute.

It is important not to overcook the custard in the bread pudding as it lends a rich creamy texture. You'll know that it's done when the center is set and the bread pudding is golden brown on top and begins to puff.

Serves 8

VANILLA SAUCE (CRÈME ANGLAISE)

A RICH AND DELICIOUS CUSTARD SAUCE THAT'S ALSO PERFECT OVER FRESH FRUITS AND BERRIES, LIGHT CAKES, AND BREAD PUDDINGS.

2 cups whole milk
1/2 cup sugar
1 vanilla bean, split lengthwise
6 large egg yolks

Combine the milk and 1/4 cup of sugar in a heavy medium saucepan. Scrape the seeds from the vanilla bean into the milk mixture, then add the bean. Bring the milk mixture to a simmer over medium-high heat. Remove from the heat.

Whisk the egg yolks and remaining 1/4 cup of sugar in a large bowl to blend. Gradually whisk in the hot milk mixture. Pour the custard into the same medium saucepan. Cook over medium-low heat until the custard thickens enough to coat the back of the spoon (do not allow the custard to boil, or the custard will curdle), stirring constantly, about 8 minutes.

Pour the custard through a fine-meshed strainer and into a medium bowl. Discard the solids. Place the bowl of custard atop a large bowl of ice water, and stir the custard until it is cool. Cover the custard, and refrigerate until it is cold.

COOK'S NOTES: It is very important to stir the custard over medium-low heat just until it thickens slightly, otherwise it will curdle.

If desired, 1 teaspoon of vanilla extract may be substituted for the vanilla bean. Just stir the vanilla extract into the custard once it is cool.

Makes 2 1/3 cups

MAIL ORDER RESOURCES

Indian Harvest Special Foods and Ingredients
1-800-294-2433
www.indianharvest.com

Kalustyans Middle Eastern and Indian Spices and Foods
123 Lexington Ave
New York, NY 10016
212-685-3451
www.kalustyans.com

Melissa's Specialty Foods and Ingredients
P. O. Box 21127
Los Angeles, California 90021
1-800-588-0151
www.melissas.com

Penzeys Ltd. Herbs, Spices, and Blends
1-800-741-7787
www.penzeys.com

Zov's Publishing LLC
17440 E. 17th street
Tustin, California 92780 USA
1-800-980-ZOVS (9687)
www.zovs.com

INDEX